CW00482529

He Who Dared
and Died

ABOUT THE AUTHOR

Gearoid O'Dowd, has spent most of his life working as a musician in Ireland and the UK. He has also lived for a time in Sweden and Denmark. In 2001 he obtained a BA Honours degree in journalism from Southampton Solent University and shortly after began working on the radical magazine, *Synergy*.

He returned to his native Galway in 2006 and began researching his uncle's life shortly after. He has a daughter Saoirse, 26, and a son Rossa, 25. This is his first book.

OXFORDSHIRE LIBRARY SERVICE	
3302539597	
Askews & Holts	06-Oct-2011
940.54232092	£19.99

He Who Dared and Died

The Life and Death of an SAS Original, Sergeant Chris O'Dowd, MM

GEAROID O'DOWD

Pen & Sword
MILITARY

First published in Great Britain in 2011 by
PEN & SWORD MILITARY
An imprint of
Pen & Sword Books Ltd
47 Church Street
Barnsley
South Yorkshire
S70 2AS

Copyright © Gearoid O'Dowd, 2011

ISBN 978-1-84884-541-1

The right of Gearoid O'Dowd to be identified as the author of this work has
been asserted by him in accordance with the Copyright, Designs and Patents
Act 1988.

A CIP catalogue record for this book is
available from the British Library

All rights reserved. No part of this book may be reproduced or transmitted in
any form or by any means, electronic or mechanical including photocopying,
recording or by any information storage and retrieval system, without
permission from the Publisher in writing.

Typeset by Concept, Huddersfield, West Yorkshire
Printed and bound in England by CPI UK

Pen & Sword Books Ltd incorporates the Imprints of Pen & Sword Aviation,
Pen & Sword Family History, Pen & Sword Maritime,
Pen & Sword Military, Pen & Sword Discovery, Wharncliffe Local History,
Wharncliffe True Crime, Wharncliffe Transport, Pen & Sword Select,
Pen & Sword Military Classics, Leo Cooper, The Praetorian Press,
Remember When, Seaforth Publishing and Frontline Publishing.

For a complete list of Pen & Sword titles please contact
PEN & SWORD BOOKS LIMITED
47 Church Street, Barnsley, South Yorkshire, S70 2AS, England
E-mail: enquiries@pen-and-sword.co.uk
Website: www.pen-and-sword.co.uk

Contents

v

List of Plates

List of Maps

Nor law, nor duty bade me fight,
Nor public men, nor cheering crowds,
A lonely impulse of delight
Drove to this tumult in the clouds;
I balanced all, brought all to mind,
The years to come seemed waste of breath,
A waste of breath the years behind
In balance with this life, this death.

'An Irish Airman Foresees his Death',
William Butler Yeats

Foreword &
Acknowledgements

For most of my life I knew nothing of my uncle's exploits during the Second World War. The only evidence of his existence in our home was a picture of him sitting on the wall outside my grandparents' house. I remember on one occasion when I was a young boy, my mother explaining that the man on Grandma's wall was my uncle Chris, who had run away to join the British Army and had been killed.

Intermittently down through the years, it nagged at my conscience that I knew so little about this man, but circumstances always prevented me acting upon it. When I finally got down to satisfying my long-held curiosity, I was astounded by what I found out, and the more I discovered about the 'man on the wall' the more I realized his story needed telling.

I am particularly indebted to Mary Maughan and the late Mick Walsh for sharing their memories of Chris, and to Mick's daughter, Teresa, for making it possible to meet him. My sincere thanks also go to Donal Carey, Principal of Gortjordan School, for all his assistance.

D.P. Cleary and Dominic Kearney, of the Irish Guards Archive, Wellington Barracks, provided me with documents and information, and Diane Flanagan's help on the Guards was invaluable (www.irish-guards.co.uk). I am also grateful to Derek Harkness and Stewart McClean of the Blair Mayne Association, Newtownards, for all their help and support. Fellow authors, Gavin Mortimer and Hamish Ross were always generous with their advice and made my task an easier one.

I would also like to thank the following: the SAS Regimental Association, The War Graves Photographic Project, Isobel Williams

(Bite Yer Legs Productions), Fr Martin Crosby (Shrule), Cha Taylor, Frank Kennedy and Joe McDonagh. A special acknowledgment to my sister, Joan, for her great patience and to my cousins, Nives (Shrule), Mary (Longford) and Chris (London) for helping me retrace our uncle's footsteps. Grateful thanks also to Gordon Stevens, Fiona Ferguson, William Deakins, Morag Storie and Martin Dillon for allowing me to use quotes, photographs and documents.

Finally, a special acknowledgment to my agents, Prizeman and Kinsella: Thank you, Patricia and Yvonne, for going that extra mile and for your unflappable belief in the book.

The following books were particularly important for my research (for full details see Bibliography): *Stirling's Men*, Gavin Mortimer; *The Originals, The Secret History of the Birth of the SAS*, Gordon Stephens; *The History of the Special Raiding Squadron: 'Paddy's Men'*, Stewart McClean; *Paddy Mayne*, Hamish Ross.

Introduction

On the evening of 6 October 1943, a group of SAS soldiers gathered to bury their fallen comrades in the gardens of a disused convent at Termoli, on the east coast of Italy. The Regiment, which was then barely two years in existence, had suffered heavy casualties and the mood of the men was sombre. Peter Davis had joined up as a debonair young officer the previous Christmas. The intervening ten months of combat had altered his dapper appearance drastically. 'Into the gathering dusk,' he recalled, 'the silent crowd of men emerged from their billets with their heads bared.' Padre Lunt read the service. Some hours earlier he had wrapped the remains of fifteen men in blankets. Despite knowing them well he had difficulty recognizing their remains, such was the carnage. The party had suffered a direct mortar hit the previous day, as they prepared to drive to the front line to help rebuff a German counter-attack. The fifteen men were killed instantly and had lain where they had fallen while the battle raged on. Three more men died later in hospital.

The SAS was in many ways a rogue element of the British Army at this stage of its existence. It had been the brainchild of Lieutenant A.D. Stirling, a Scots-Catholic of impeccable pedigree. His father was an MP and his maternal grandfather was the 16th Baron Lovat. Stirling's soldiering however, did little to inspire confidence in his superiors. He had been sent down from Cambridge, and he was better known for his drinking binges and gambling than for any fighting talent. On his graduation from Sandhurst he was described as an 'irresponsible and unremarkable' soldier who neglected his duties, disobeyed orders and spent his time partying. He was posted to Cairo in 1941, and after a night on the town he would often see out his hangover in the military hospital, cadging shots of oxygen from the nurses and returning late for duty. Few who knew him would have predicted that he would create a unit that was to become the most famous fighting force in the world, changing the face of modern warfare in the process. But while stationed in Cairo he was hospitalized with injuries incurred while he was off-duty. During his recuperation (his superiors believed he was malingering) he hit upon his idea: an elite force, made up of small units, capable of infiltrating behind enemy lines and inflicting strategic damage. They would train to kill quickly and silently and would operate mainly by night, usually without army uniform or insignia.

Although well connected, Stirling knew he would be up against what he liked to call 'the fossilized shits' among the 'top brass', in trying to get his idea across. He dismissed any attempt to speak to them through the usual channels, which he felt would be futile. Instead he opted to evade the sentries at HQ by scaling the perimeter fence. Ignoring shouts to halt he arrived at the door of Major General Neil Ritchie, a progressive soldier who had shot grouse with his father and who, he felt, would give him a sympathetic hearing. Incredibly, his plan was accepted and a week later he was given three months to organize and train his new unit.

The Special Air Service was up and running by November 1941. Although the first mission was a disaster, they went on to wreak havoc on Rommel's army in the deserts of North Africa, blowing up hundreds of planes and destroying railway lines deep inside enemy lines. Hitler considered the unit a sufficient threat to his ambitions for world dominance that he ordered the immediate execution of any SAS members, upon capture. Undaunted, these men proceeded to successfully spearhead the invasion of Sicily. By now it was late 1943, the Italians had surrendered apart from a few pockets of Fascist sympathizers, and the Allied objective was to create hell along the Gustav Line in order to force the Germans to reinforce it with fresh troops. Meanwhile, under cover of this distraction, preparations were made for D-Day.

Many of those gathered around the gravesides in Termoli that evening would become casualties themselves during the fierce fighting that followed in France and Germany. Others would survive and return to civilian life. The survivors preferred not to talk of their heroic service and the SAS became shrouded in secrecy, with the identity of its members known to few. Indeed the general public would only become aware of the existence of the Regiment after its controversial deployment in Northern Ireland in 1972 and in particular when live pictures of one SAS operation, the storming of the Iranian Embassy siege in London, were televised all over the world in 1980. Though the fellowship of the veterans remained steadfast in the intervening years, they waited until 1985 to put their adventures on public record. In these interviews, which were not released until 2005, they shunned tags such as 'heroes', preferring to consider themselves ordinary men who had simply done something extraordinary for a few years of their lives. The common denominator among them was an abhorrence of petty army discipline, a longing for adventure and a belief that they were laying their lives on the line for a just cause. They came from all walks of life and all sorts of places.

Among the casualties being laid to rest on that fateful evening was Lance Sergeant Christopher O'Dowd, MM, an ex-Irish Guard and an SAS veteran at the age of twenty-three. He came from a small farm, 4 miles outside the village of Shrule, on the Galway-Mayo border in the west of Ireland. He was also my uncle. This book is dedicated to his sacrifice.

Chapter One

Early Days

Christopher O'Dowd was born in the family home at Cahernabruck, Shrule, on 6 September 1920. At around the same time Jack Dempsey was knocking out Billy Miske for the World Heavyweight boxing title in the first bout to be broadcast worldwide on radio. The Black River, which flows through the west side of the village, divides the Counties of Galway and Mayo. Although for logistical reasons its postal address has always been County Galway, Shrule is geographically in Mayo. While this can cause confusion for outsiders, the people have never been in doubt as to where their loyalties lie. The Shrule sports teams play within the Mayo leagues, and local brothers Anthony and Connor Mortimer have been inspirational players on the Mayo Gaelic football team in recent years. Christy, as he was always known, was the ninth in line of twelve children born to James and Sarah (née O'Sullivan) O'Dowd at their 40-acre farm, 4 miles outside the village. He had seven older brothers to look up to, but was especially close to Mary Catherine, his older sister by two years. Michael, the eldest was already ten when Christy was born. By the time he was four, Christy had two younger sisters, Delia and Nora, as well as a baby brother Gerard, who had cerebral palsy (though at that time such conditions remained undiagnosed). While the family was not exceptionally large for those days, it must have been a busy house with twelve little ones to nourish and nurture.

Ireland was a country in political turmoil at this time. The dust had barely settled from the Great War, which took the lives of 40,000 Irishmen. A further 200,000 people lost their lives to the Spanish influenza, which devastated the country during the years 1918 and 1919. The War of Independence was now in full swing and the dreaded Black and Tans were wreaking their particular brand of havoc across the land two months after Christy was born. By the time Christy was a year old Ireland had gained her place among the nations of the earth, although the violence continued with the disaster that was the Civil War. Nevertheless, when he took his first tentative steps to the local school on 5 May 1925, the country had settled down somewhat.

Gortjordan National School was about 2 miles from the O'Dowds' house by road, but a short cut through the fields, bare-footed in summer, could halve the journey. James O' Dowd's sister, Margaret, was married to Thomas Maughan and they lived in the neighbouring cottage. Their daughter Mary remembers Christy coming a cropper when he attempted to shorten the journey home even more. It was a hard winter and the local pond had frozen over. Christy, ignoring the warnings of his fellow scholars, decided to try skating. The inevitable happened as he approached the centre and that could have been the end of his story, but he eventually dragged himself back to dry land, soaked but still seeing the funny side. The school was divided into boys and girls, each section having two rooms, and there were four teachers in all. It had been built at the turn of the century and stands next door to the local church to this day.

It seems unlikely that Christy enjoyed school. In an era when corporal punishment was the order of the day, nobody but a masochist could look forward to a school day. Punishment was meted out by means of an ash plant, and talking or laughing during class could merit up to six 'slaps' on each hand. Failure to produce homework or any hint of insubordination was dealt with severely. Those incurring the wrath of a grumpy teacher could have their ears and hair pulled, or become the recipients of a few well-placed 'thumps'. Perhaps because of the initial shock, Christy's school records show he only attended on fifty-eight days of his first year in Infants, although he appears to have taken to schooling fairly well after that. Apart from having been kept back for a year in Second Class, his attendance record is good.

During these years and up until the 1970s it was normal for farmers' children, boys and girls, to miss a lot of school time, as and when they were needed to help with the harvest, tilling and so on. But it seems from the records that after the initial shock Christy preferred to take his chances with the schoolmaster, rather than spend the day on the farm. He was considered to be 'very brainy' by his peers, but had a tendency to exasperate his teachers by seeming to know all the answers. According to Mick Walsh, who was four years his junior, the master would have been a much happier man if Christy had stayed a bit quieter. Nor did he confine his torment of the man to inside the classroom. One day, while engaged in some horseplay in the yard, Christy announced to all and sundry that he would be the hare, and they would play the hounds. With that he jumped the wall and headed over the fields with 'the hunt' in quick pursuit. Needless to say there was hell to pay when the master finally rounded up the culprits. Those who heeded his furious shouts to return were spared the worst of his anger but the rest, including the ringleader, were made to pay dearly.

The typical school day began at 9.30 am, with an allowance made for latecomers until 10 o'clock. During the winter months each scholar brought a sod of turf for the classroom fire, unless their parents had made alternative arrangements with the school by paying in cash or donating a cartload of turf to cover the season. Despite the open hearth the children's hands often went numb with cold, rendering them unable to write. They wrote with ink, the pen consisting of a steel nib attached to a wooden handle, and lived in constant fear of blotting the copybook with a stray drop of ink. They sat at long benches, six to a bench, surrounded by various maps and holy pictures. There was great emphasis put on Religious Instruction in the early years, with annual examinations on the Catechism. Reading and writing in both Irish and English, and Mathematics, were also considered important. Many of the older generation spoke Irish fluently, so their children had a head start. In later years Irish history and Geography were also given a lot of time on the curriculum. Lunch was from 1.00 to 1.30 pm and would typically consist of bread and jam or cheese, currant cake and a bottle of milk. There was a well across the road to supply water and the toilet was outdoors and basic.

The bell went to end the day at 3.30 pm, whereupon the boys were always let out first. A mad dash usually ensued with scholars eager to leave the scene of their daily confinement. As an infant, Mick Walsh was smaller than the rest, and would sometimes get left behind by the older boys going his way home. In later years he recalled how Christy would stay back to walk with him, until his house was within sight. The journey home was full of distractions and in good weather it was often only the pangs of hunger that would finally send the children indoors. Youngsters picked black-berries and hazelnuts, raided orchards and birds' nests and interacted with nature on a daily basis. Treats such as confectionery were just the stuff of dreams to these young people. Perhaps a visiting uncle or aunt would bring a bag of 'Peggy's legs' on a rare occasion. These were caramel-coloured sticks of candy and, along with Cleeve's slab toffee, were much sought after. At home there were usually chores to be done, especially for the older children. Helping on the farm with the feeding and herding of animals and working in the fields alongside the grown-ups was common practice for children, and essential to their parents. In an era without any electricity or running water, life was hard and there were always chores to be done. Christy took hard work in his stride and it helped him grow to be an exceptionally strong young man.

Back in the grown-up world, nationalistic fervour was taking hold. The General Election of 1932 swept Eamon de Valera's Fianna Fáil into power and he promptly refused to reimburse the British government for loans they had granted Irish tenant farmers, in order to help them buy their land from the British landlords. As part of the Agreement, which gave Southern Ireland self-government in 1921, the Irish negotiators promised to collect these loans. When De Valera reneged on the deal, Britain imposed a 20 per cent tax on all Irish imports. De Valera responded in kind, but it was always going to be an uneven contest. Ireland depended almost exclusively on its neighbour as a market for exports, such as they were – at that time mainly livestock and dairy produce. Certain factions of Dev's party borrowed Jonathan Swift's slogan, 'Burn everything British but their coal', to get their point across, but the following five years were hard for the farming community of the new Free State. With rural households feeling the pinch, they had little to spend on non-essentials, and the towns and factories suffered in turn. To confound matters further, emigration to America and Britain no longer seemed an option for the hard-pressed, as the Great Depression took hold.

Indeed, the situation in the United States affected many poorer families due to their reliance on assistance from relatives already living there. Britain, in turn, was also in a slump and suffering mass unemployment. Nevertheless, those who made a living from the land in Ireland had the advantage of being almost self-sufficient. Coal was needed mainly by the railways and factories, while most homes burned turf and timber, which were both plentiful. Christy's father was an enterprising farmer and used what land he had to the maximum. He raised cattle, pigs and poultry and grew wheat and potatoes along with the usual vegetables. Ploughing and harrowing was done by real horsepower and tractors were still a wish for the future. A slaughter man was called out when it was time to kill a pig. The poor pig's squeals would be heard for miles, as it tried to avoid the inevitable. The bacon was then cut into joints and hung up in the chimney of the open hearth, to be smoked. The lads would often convert the pig's bladder to use as a football. As the older lads grew they became expert shots, and there was plenty of pheasant, partridge, wild duck or goose and rabbit to embellish the kitchen table. Salmon, trout and eel were also in abundance from the Black River.

Sarah's niece, Mary Maughan, remembers her as a hard-working and exceptionally resourceful woman. She had spent her formative years in New York and returned to Mayo with her parents as a young girl. As a result, she spoke with the barest hint of an American drawl all her life. Arriving back to the West of Ireland must have been a huge culture shock for the young woman but by the time she married James she was well ensconced in the local life and customs. Some essentials were bought in the village or from the travelling shop, which arrived weekly. Tea, sugar, flour, beef and tobacco were the basics on any shopping list. All the cooking was done on the open fire and with such a large family to feed that would be a full-time job for most mortals. Sarah, however, was made of sterner stuff. On top of cooking, washing and mending clothes, she fed and milked the cows, churned butter, and helped with the sowing and harvesting. Most of the children's clothes were hand-made. Sarah and the girls would knit jumpers, socks and so on, and many houses had a spinning wheel. The local tailor made suits for special occasions such as a First Holy Communion. Sarah also got the older lads to make a mobility cart for Gerard and it made a big difference in his life. He was now able to accompany his brothers and sisters on all their outdoor adventures. First cousin, Mary Maughan remembers how Sarah kept her youngest spotlessly clean, which can't have been easy given his condition.

When the evenings closed in, and the farming chores and home-work were completed, the strains of a hornpipe or reel could often be heard emanating from the busy house. James was an accom-plished flute player, a fact that had not escaped Sarah when she first came across him apparently, and they both liked nothing more than a good music session. O'Dowd's was what was known as a 'gathering house' and the local musicians would often meet there for a session. Intermingled with more traditional airs, the songs of John McCormack or local favourites such as 'Moonlight in Mayo' were often sung. When the musicians and dancers were exhausted, someone would tell a story. These were often tales handed down through the generations and steeped in Celtic mysticism. The exploits of Cú Chulainn and the sad plight of the Children of Lir would have been familiar to Christy and his siblings, and would undoubtedly have fired their imaginations. Another favourite pastime was card playing. Twenty-Five was the most popular game and was a great test of guile, especially when played with a partner. As Christy grew up he would have been allowed to stay up with the others, especially in the school holidays and during those years he developed a love of singing and music generally. This was to stand him in good stead in later life for many a campfire singing session. His interest in guns at this time was also apparent to those who knew him – Mary can recall her older cousin cutting out pictures of rifles and pistols from the magazines of the day. His big brothers would also have taught him to use a shotgun as soon as he could hold one: all the lads were expert marksmen, especially Seamus and John.

However, Christy was soon to learn how cruel life could be for in late 1932, while he was still a young lad of twelve himself, his little brother Gerard passed away, aged just eight. While his parents and older siblings may have been somewhat prepared for the tragedy, it must have come as a terrible shock to the younger ones. There can be little doubt it left its mark on Christy's character. He had learned of the fragility of life so early on in his own. Nevertheless, the family endeavoured to carry on as best they could, in an era that was later to become known worldwide as 'the Hungry Thirties'. Having buried her youngest child, the redoubtable Sarah dealt with her grief by busying herself around the house and farm. There was simply no time to wallow in melancholy. The housekeeping was becoming slightly less demanding as her children grew and became more helpful. As the years passed, the older siblings began to move away and make their own mark on the world. Paddy, Martin and Joe had already moved to England and Mary emigrated to New York soon after her eighteenth birthday. The eldest son, Michael would stay on to inherit the farm as was usual. Seamus, John and

Tom were gainfully employed and seemed determined to make a life for themselves at home in Ireland. Meanwhile Christy was growing up to be a strapping young man. He spent his last day at Gortjordan School on 8 February 1936. He had already turned sixteen and was now ready to take on the world.

He managed to get a job in the nearest big town without much delay. McTigue's and Co., Ballinrobe, was a hardware, ironmongery and grocery shop of long establishment and Christy became their latest recruit. Although the job itself didn't fill him with much enthusiasm, he revelled in his newfound freedom. He could now contribute to the family coffers and still have some money left to enjoy his teenage years. While his wages as a shop assistant would have been meagre, he managed to buy a racing bike with a little help from his parents. Christy soon became a familiar sight speeding along the road on his way to or from Ballinrobe, a full 12 miles. There was little danger from traffic apart from the odd commercial vehicle. Private cars were still a rarity and could be afforded only by the professional classes. But the big town, with a population of 1,500 people, held more attraction than Shrule. It boasted a cinema, dance hall and several lively pubs and while money was scarce the young locals of the period were intent on enjoying their youth.

He was now also in a position to buy his own clothes for the first time. The drapery shops of the town could satisfy a young man's every whim, provided of course he could afford it. Tall, dark and ruggedly handsome, Christy now cut quite a dash as he strolled the streets. He had no shortage of female admirers, and was much in demand as a partner at the local dances. Cousin Mary recalls many of her pals having a fancy for him, but thoughts of settling down anytime soon with some local girl were a long way from his mind. There was a great big world out there and Christy was determined to have a good look around.

As an intelligent young man, he would have been well aware of the political crisis that was engulfing the world, especially in Europe. The rise of Fascism in Italy, Spain, and Germany would not have escaped his attention. The Spanish Civil War, which started shortly after Christy left school, was grinding on with no end in sight. Hitler, now firmly in control of Germany was re-arming at a frightening rate. He sent the Luftwaffe to Franco's aid and it proved an ideal testing ground for his air force. German bombers reduced the city of Guernica to rubble and later introduced the concept of

11

carpet-bombing to the world at Barcelona. These atrocities were reported internationally, but the Pathé Newsreels shown at local cinemas would have really brought the reality home to people.

While Oswald Mosley was organizing his particular band of fascists in Britain, Ireland had her own flirtation with the latest political movement. Eoin O'Duffy's 'Blue Shirts' were intent on following the example of their heroes, Mussolini, Hitler and Franco. O'Duffy was Catholic with a capital C and detested communism. He was an ex-Chief of Staff of the Free State Army and had succeeded in recruiting many of his ex-solders. He organized well-attended rallies throughout the country, which were frequently disrupted by elements of the IRA and often ended in violence. Ironically, only a few years later, the IRA were harbouring Nazi spies and attempting to solicit an arms deal with Hitler. In 1936, O'Duffy sent 700 of his men to fight with Franco. They were blessed by the Catholic hierarchy as they left Dublin Bay. Meanwhile, a band of 300 Irish communists also departed the shores to join the Republican 'International Brigade', but for them there was little fanfare. De Valera, no doubt, would have been glad to see the back of O'Duffy for a while, as he had seen him as a genuine threat. De Valera, in the meantime, was now busy promoting his Nationalist agenda.

While De Valera's slogan, 'Burn everything British but their coal' was not original, it served to illustrate perfectly what he expected of the Irish people. He was determined to shake off the yoke of colonialism, quickly and completely. Irish culture and language were encouraged and those who held on to the old Imperialist trappings were often treated with scorn. The thousands of men who had returned home having survived the Great War were now made to feel like second-class citizens in their own country. Far from being seen as heroes, they were frequently jibed at for fighting on the side of the old enemy, and letting down the rebels of 1916. Christy, it seems, was seeing the bigger picture. Chamberlain's policy of appeasement towards Hitler was a failed one, and the more astute thinkers realized the world was heading for another major war. Christy was stuck in a job he didn't like while most of his older siblings had gone far away. He particularly missed Mary, his favourite, and the prospect of his joining her in New York was discussed at home at one stage. However, the unexpected demise of a cow put paid to that idea. Christy was now expressing a need for adventure in his conversations with friends and the romance of soldiering appealed to him increasingly. Yet he succeeded in keeping his ambitions a secret at home and both James and Sarah remained blissfully ignorant up to the last. As far as it can be ascertained, he collected his last pay packet from McTigue's towards the end of the summer of 1938 and, after hanging around for a few weeks, made his move. With Sarah's nagging probably still ringing in his ears he sold the racing bike to a near neighbour, Paddy Brennan from Ballybocaugh.

The next day he packed a bag and slipped away, heading for the nearest railway station. At Claremorris he boarded the train for Dublin. In his pocket was a ticket for the boat to Holyhead and a little money. No doubt he felt guilty about stealing away without saying goodbye to his mother and father, but all that could be put right when he returned. He would have caught his first sight of a city as they passed through the capital on route to the docks. From Holyhead he travelled to Manchester to visit Paddy, who was now well established and in a position to help his young brother find his feet. Christy however seemed determined to head to London where Martin had recently moved. He was fixed on the notion of soldiering and intent on joining the British Army. Needless to say he received little encouragement from Paddy for this idea. After a few days, and with best wishes (and no doubt a few bob) from his elder brother, he boarded the train yet again. This time he was bound for the Big Smoke.

Chapter Two

Norway with the 'Micks'

Dublin had flashed by in a matter of minutes. Manchester had been well worth a look through the smog, but neither could compare with the magnificence of the English capital. Arriving in Victoria for the first time, Christy would have experienced a cornucopia of emotions. To a young lad from rural Ireland the bustle must have seemed incredible. He would have seen images of the famous landmarks at the cinema in Ballinrobe, but now he was here for real, and the world was waiting for him to make his next move. Any feelings of homesickness he may have had were displaced when he met up with Martin, now living in Heston, West London. Within weeks, Christy was gainfully employed as a live-in barman in Victoria. Martin himself was on the building sites, but it seems Christy had no particular desire to go down that road. It was at this time also that he became seriously involved with a girlfriend. Unfortunately, there is no one alive today who can remember her name or anything about her. So, things were beginning to look up for Christy. He was living in one of the most exiting cities in the world, doing a job he liked, with a sweetheart thrown into the bargain. He had also written home and had been forgiven for running away. It must have seemed as if good fortune had singled him out for special treatment.

The Irish Republican Army, however, had other ideas. As the world entered the fateful year of 1939, the IRA announced that they would begin a bombing campaign on mainland Britain. On 16 January the first of these bombs exploded in London, Birmingham and Manchester. Two weeks later, devices in the left luggage offices of Tottenham Court Road and Leicester Square tube stations caused devastation and panic. Thankfully, there was no loss of life incurred in either of these incidents, but no doubt life became more awkward for Christy. Suddenly, the genial young barman with the charming brogue would have been seen by many of the locals in a totally different light. Like many thousands of his compatriots who came both before and after, he would have had to bear the brunt of the British people's anger. The IRA came and went as they pleased, but the Irish who lived and worked in Britain paid a price.

Meanwhile, on the global front, Neville Chamberlain's policy of appeasement towards Hitler was becoming increasingly unpopular. Following the annexation of Czechoslovakia in early March, he had promised to support Poland if she were threatened. All the talk was now of war – everyone knew it was coming, it was just a question of when. In April, Chamberlain introduced the Military Training Act. The British Army had shed much of its strength since the Great War and now numbered not much more than 200,000 men. The Act required men between the ages of twenty and twenty-one to register for six months' army training, but stopped short of all-out conscription. Those involved in 'reserved occupations' were exempt. Occupations considered important enough for exemption included dockers, miners, merchant seamen, farmers and utility workers. There was every possibility of an extension of the Act to include a broader age group in the near future and as a result there was a sudden rise in applications for the 'reserved' jobs throughout the country. Many young Irishmen spent the war years down the mines or as merchant seamen, while many more went home when it became apparent that Ireland was to remain neutral. The new Act made little impression on Christy however; he had already made up his mind. As a young boy he had dreamt of being a soldier. It's hard to say what planted the notion in his head, as there was no history of militarism in the family whatsoever. Perhaps he was impressed by stories from veterans of the First World War whom he may have befriended as a lad. It seems more likely, however, that his desire for combat was nurtured through reading war stories of the time, and of course the cinema. It seems safe to assume, in any case, that Christy had decided on his plan of action long before he sold his bike and headed for Holyhead. Paddy, Joe and Martin had all done their best to discourage him, to no avail. Nor, it appears, could his girlfriend dissuade him. He was determined to fight Hitler and was only one of 70,000 Southern Irishmen to do so.

Christy enlisted as an Irish Guard on 5 May 1939, aged eighteen years and nine months. As a full-grown young man he weighed in at 143 pounds and his height was 5 feet 11 inches. He would have had only to walk a short distance from the pub to Wellington Barracks in order to sign on the dotted line, but it was an action that was to have enormous implications for his future life. Having given his notice at the pub, he reported for training the following week and was assigned to the 1st Battalion. He was then sent to complete twenty-eight weeks basic training at Caterham Barracks, outside London. Upon arrival each man drew down two battle-dress uniforms from the quartermaster. They also got a denim uniform for heavy training and two caps, one of which was the proper peaked cap of the Guards. Under the direction of the squad sergeant, the men then swore the Oath of Allegiance to King and Country. They next learned the history and tradition of the Regiment. They were the monarch's household troops, the sergeant told them, and had the unique responsibility of guarding Buckingham Palace. The men were then given their 'swabbing jobs' for the week. They learned to polish boots and buttons, to shave quickly in cold water, to fold blankets, lay out kit and a hundred other things that may have seemed petty at the time.

There were three things a soldier had to have on his person at all times. They were his AB647 form, which contained his enlistment details and pay book, an emergency wound dressing and his identity discs. Failure to produce these items could result in being entered into the record book for punishment. The following weeks were filled with seemingly endless parades, drills, marches, and weapons training. The men were also lectured on enemy arms and techniques. Those accustomed to privacy in their previous lives were soon rudely awakened. They ate and slept together and took communal baths. The various drills and assault courses helped to bond the recruits and Christy would have had no trouble identifying the regional accents of his new comrades. Ironically, while these men were readying themselves to protect world democracy, their fellow countrymen in the IRA were still intent on terrorizing the civilian population. The worst atrocity occurred in Coventry on 25 August, when a bomb killed five people and injured over a hundred. But the men had precious little time to dwell on such issues. The following week Germany invaded Poland and Britain declared war as a result. Less than three weeks later Christy and his fellow recruits were attending their passing-out parade at Caterham. Those who had survived the training had been toughened up both physically and mentally. They were fighting fit by the time they returned to Wellington Barracks.

The 1st Battalion were now absorbed into the 24th Guards Brigade along with the 2nd Battalion South Welsh Borderers and the 1st Battalion Scots Guards. The 2nd Battalion Irish Guards were also at the barracks. Christy now found himself amongst experienced fighters for the first time. There were a good few Guardsmen who had fought in Spain in the International Brigade. In addition, some men had seen service in Palestine in 1938. There were even a few ex-IRA men serving under assumed names at that time, it is now believed. Those in the 1st who had already done service knew their Scottish namesakes well. The Borderers on the other hand had just returned from a lengthy tour of India and were a bit of an unknown quantity.

This was a period that would become known as the 'Phoney War' for obvious reasons. When Chamberlain declared war, he sent the British Expeditionary Force to France to help defend her. However, the expected full-scale battle for Europe did not ensue and there was even talk of a peace agreement. In any event, it became apparent that the Guards would be going nowhere, until the New Year at the earliest. Christy would have had a good Christmas leave spent in the company of his girlfriend and brothers, including Joe who arrived from Nottingham. As 1940 turned the corner the government announced the rationing of basics such as butter and sugar and the people braced themselves for future hardships to come. On 1 April, Colonel Faulkner, Commanding Officer of the 1st Battalion, received orders that his men were likely to be on the move in the near future. The rumours amongst the troops began immediately, with France being touted as the most likely destination. In the event, their speculation was to prove very wide of the mark. Three days later, the troops were inspected at Wellington Barracks by the king, a sure indicator, if one were needed, of impending embarkation. All leave was cancelled and packing began in earnest the very next day. On the 8th, the Bren-gun carriers were loaded on to flats and sent northwards from King's Cross station. The next day the Scots Guards were also sent north.

The guessing game continued as the excitement grew and April 10th was now seen as the likely date for departure. On the evening of the 10th the Company Commandants barked out their orders: 'We wear "full Christmas Tree Order – Change of Quarters" with additions. British warms with a haversack slung on each side.' The battalion then paraded on the square for a full kit inspection in their brand new battle-dress. They were watched by an audience of the 2nd Battalion and the families from the married quarters. When the Green Line buses arrived to transport the men, the secret was out. On the sides were scrawled slogans such as 'The North Pole Express', 'See the Midnight Sun', and 'To Norway'. So Norway it was to be. As the men were piped from barracks, they were greeted by shouts of 'Keep Your Head Down Mick' from their pals in the 2nd Battalion. They replied with quips such as, 'Get back to the Naafi, this country needs real soldiers now!' At 8.00 pm, amidst the usual tearful farewells, the troops left Euston station bound for Greenock.

The journey north turned into a little adventure all of its own. The top brass seemed determined to see off 'the Micks' in style. Each carriage was given a crate of beer, while the officers travelling in first class availed themselves of double magnums of champagne. On arrival, the battalion somewhat the worse for wear, marched straight to the King George V dock and boarded the *Monarch of Bermuda*. She was a three-funnel ex-cruise ship that had already transported a load of Canadian troops across the Atlantic. Soon after the Guards had boarded, it was discovered they had 'mislaid' some of their equipment. The dockers, taking advantage of the occasion, had relieved the supply carriages of various items – including the entire stock of binoculars. On the afternoon of 11 April, at 3.00 pm, the *Monarch of Bermuda* set sail under the Battalion flag. The men clustered at the rails as the ship sailed up the Clyde for, what would be for many, a last look. The 1st Battalion South Wales Borderers were on another ship of the convoy, while the Scots Guards had gone on ahead. The men were immediately issued with Arctic clothing for the climate that awaited them. Here, the Army didn't scrimp. They had engaged, as advisors to the Ministry of Supply, no less than F.S. Smythe of the Everest expedition and Ernest Shackleton, son of the famous Arctic explorer. Each man received a sheepskin coat weighing over 50 lbs, a quilted sleeping bag, two pullovers, eight pairs of socks, three pairs of snow gloves, two leather jerkins and a white fur hat, which the men quickly nicknamed 'the baby bearskin', given its resemblance to their own ceremonial headgear. Chris had more clothes than he had ever had in his life and the main adventure was yet to begin. Every soldier on board had two kit bags stuffed with supplies and the men were constantly tripping over them in the confusion.

When they were well at sea Colonel Faulkner summoned his officers to his stateroom to issue the orders from London. The men in the room had some idea already of what lay ahead of them. The Allies had known for some time that the Germans were preparing for an invasion, but were unsure of the target. The British Navy had mined Norwegian waters on 8 April to prevent the Germans evading Allied blockades. The Norwegians took umbrage at this and saw it as a violation of their neutrality. They had little time to protest however, as the next day the Germans poured into Denmark, and from there into Norway without too much opposition. The regular Norwegian Army was ill equipped and tiny. Their Navy consisted of two warships and a few submarines and there was no Air Force to speak of, in a country that had lived in peace for over a hundred years. As the invasion proceeded, the Germans announced that they had taken such steps as were necessary to 'eliminate the north of Europe from British plans for extending the war and to safeguard peace and protect the weak.' Norway was strategically of great importance to both sides. Whoever controlled it had access to the North Atlantic. If the German navy could seize control of the ports, they would be in a position to launch attacks on the Allied Arctic convoys. The country was also rich in raw materials such as iron ore and timber and the Germans were intent on taking full advantage, in order to boost their war machine. The Colonel informed his officers that his brigade's mission was to land at Narvik and to secure the peninsula. 'Unfortunately,' he said, 'the Germans are still firmly in possession of Narvik, and all the maps are on another ship.' After some deliberations they were finally redirected to land at Harstad, 40 miles further up the coast.

As the convoy sped northwards, the vast array of vessels must have been a reassuring sight for any man having second thoughts. They had four other liners for company, the *Empress of Australia*, the *Reino del Pacifico* and two Polish ships, the *Batory* and the *Chobry*. Twelve destroyers protected the edges of the convoy, which also contained three cruisers and a net-laying ship, from U-boat attack. A huge flying boat hovered overhead. Later three of the liners broke away with an escort and sailed towards Namsos. After four days plain sailing the *Monarch of Bermuda* rounded the northernmost tip of the Lofoten Islands and sailed down Vaggs Fjord in the middle of the night. The men's first impressions of what was to be their new home could have been better. The barren rocky walls of the fjord seemed to stretch endlessly up to the heavens, while the snow covered everything else. The whole place looked very cold and uninviting.

They were now some 200 miles inside the Arctic Circle. Every so often they came across a fishing village, its fragile-looking jetties packed with small twin-mast fishing boats. Flocks of eider duck took to the sky, to avoid the commotion. Suddenly a destroyer rushed past, rocking the narrow water. 'We got one!' the crew were shouting. They had indeed sunk a U-boat and picked up the survivors. More importantly, they had also picked up the U-boat's log. From the log they discovered the rendezvous of the enemy submarine flotilla. When they eventually turned up so did the Navy, and they sank the lot. Finally, they reached Harstad and were led into the harbour by the cruiser *Aurora*. Some locals stood on the waterside by their houses, waving towards the long line of ships. The men watched and waved back. Several of the little fishing boats had set out towards them, all flying the Norwegian flag and lurching in the heavy swell. Their home-made engines spluttered incessantly as they pulled alongside. Some officers had now landed, and having spoken to the Norwegians they fired a Very light to give the all clear. The destroyer *Electra* then drew up alongside the *Bermuda* to disembark the men of the 1st. Clad in their Arctic coats, pullovers and snow gloves, they were ready and anxious to get ashore. With the *Electra* full, the fishing craft, or 'little puffers' as the men were now calling them, took off the remainder of the men. Many had trouble adapting to this new mode of transport as they slid all over the snow-covered decks, but without major mishap they were all billeted in the local school and soon settled in to their surroundings. The date was 15 April, and they were now in control of the most northerly post of the North-West Expeditionary Force.

They soon realized the Germans were well aware of their presence. Over the captured radio station at Oslo, they heard themselves referred to as 'unemployed and hired volunteers'. This did not go down well of course; the Irish Guards preferred to think of themselves as mercenaries. Any false sense of security they may have felt was shattered five days later when the Germans left the town in smoking ruins. The Luftwaffe timed their attack for optimum effect, striking as the remainder of the expeditionary force, clerks, signallers and so on, were still arriving. Colonel Faulkner was in conference at the time and he and the officers emerged to witness the chaos. The little timber houses, built on light stilts to raise them from the snow, hadn't stood a chance. The bombers returned every morning for the next week, but the battalion was well away by then. They were ordered on to Liland, a little fishing village in Bogen Bay, northwest of Narvik. There was also a British Brigade at Nasmos and another at Andalsnes in the centre of the country. If these forces could clear the Narvik area, the British could then sweep south and clear the Germans out of Norway completely. The idea did not sit particularly well with Colonel Faulkner, however. He suspected that the forces further south were badly armed and would be useless against the enemy's unhindered use of the air. He had a premonition that he would not see out the end of the campaign and insisted on having the Battalion chaplain, Father Cavanagh, present at all the conferences he had with his superior commanders. 'I want you there, Father, so you can tell them at home what happened,' he would say. Apart from himself, the only men with First World War experience were his second-in-command, Major C.L.J. Bowen and the quartermaster. Major Bowen had also served in the Royal Flying Corps and was well aware of the threat of unopposed air power, especially under conditions of perpetual daylight, as was now the situation. In Narvik itself the German Third Mountain Division were firmly in control with a force of 4,000 men, most of whom had seen action in Poland. Colonel Faulkner had witnessed the wholesale slaughter of troops due to ineptitude at the top in the Great War, and he was determined not to allow this to happen to the Irish Guards. Meanwhile, the men did their utmost to entertain themselves. They took skiing instruction from the locals and also tried their hands at tobogganing. They were popular with the locals and many a 'Big Irelander' as they were called, would leave a sweetheart behind when they eventually left Norway.

Finally, on 22 April, the order came to attack Narvik. Churchill, as head of the Admiralty, was pushing for immediate action. However, there were differing opinions as to the best method of handling what would be the first amphibious landing by British troops since the disaster of Gallipoli, twenty-five years earlier. The hope was that a naval bombardment of the port would give sufficient cover to afford the Guards an opportunity to land successfully. As it transpired, they would never find out. Amid howling gales and with snow and frozen spray stinging their faces, the 'Micks' embarked on the *Vindictive* the next day, but no sooner had they left than an order came down to cancel the operation. The ship was devoid of ship-to-shore radio and although attempts were made to contact her with torches, the *Vindictive* sailed on. Just when it seemed that Christy and his comrades would face their first real taste of combat however, the Navy cancelled the operation as the weather worsened. It seems unlikely that the men were too disappointed. On top of the weather they would have had to land one platoon at a time, as there was only one landing craft available. The port was also well defended and heavily mined. Back in Bogen Bay the men did their best to keep up morale after this latest escapade.

An impressive armada was now collecting in the port and on occasion it was necessary to take stock of the situation. With this in mind, a Walrus seaplane was despatched one morning and began flying low over the water, only to be greeted by a sudden burst of Bren gun fire. 'Who's that in charge of that post?' asked Colonel Faulkner. The culprit turned out to be Lance Corporal Ludlow, otherwise known as 'Twenty-to-Four' because of the angle of his feet. After he had been marched into Commanding Officer's Orders next morning, a group of sympathetic friends waited for him to emerge. 'What did you get?' 'A reprimand,' he replied. 'What for?' 'Missing a low-flying admiral.' It turned out the plane had contained Lord Cork and Orrery, no less, head of the entire Norwegian operation.

The 'Micks' now settled in once more to a period of leisure. Occasionally there were fatigues to be done like the unloading of provisions or constructing bomb shelters. But for the most part the men passed lazy days fishing and swimming. They still had the Luftwaffe to contend with, but they had grown accustomed to the sudden raids at this stage. Outside of this relative calm however, the Germans were making rapid progress in central Norway. Their superior forces had eventually caused the survivors of the April 17 landings to evacuate. They had fought bravely but could no longer hold their defensive positions. In a brilliant campaign, the Germans had won control of the most vital part of Norway within three weeks. Not resting on their laurels they continued onwards relentlessly and took Nasmos, 1,000 miles further north, on 4 May. Five days later as they continued the push, they learned that Britain had a new Prime Minister. Amid mounting criticism, Chamberlain had resigned and Winston Churchill became the new leader. He immediately injected a new sense of urgency into the War Cabinet and while his First World War record had not covered him in glory, people were prepared to row in behind him and give him the benefit of the doubt for now at least. New orders were finally received on 13 May. The battalions were to sail south to reinforce the fragile line of defence that was endeavouring to slow the German advance. The three battalions were to leave at four-hour intervals, the Scots Guards in the morning, followed by the Irish who were to sail in the *Chobry* and finally the Borderers in the *Effingham*.

The operation got off to an ominous start. With the Scots away, the men of the 1st were being transported out to their ship by three old riverboats and a flat-bottomed barge. Along with the men and usual kit, they were carrying three times the normal amount of reserve ammunition. The steamers were unseaworthy and so top-heavy that the men were used as ballast in the waterlogged holds. The barge was also dangerously overloaded. All three vessels finally arrived alongside the *Chobry* that evening, at 1700 hrs. She was a new Polish motor ship, and was at least comfortable and well pro-visioned. But no preparations had been made to load the battalion and it was three in the morning by the time the last of the men and ammunition were on board. They were now anchored alongside several other warships , sitting ducks to an enemy air-strike. Captain Brian O'Neill had waited all day for the order to move. At 1800 hrs a Liaison Officer finally arrived with orders to sail immediately. He brought no further orders and only a vague apology. Captain O'Neill dispatched him with a flea in his ear: 'Five hours you've kept us waiting. During that time we've been bombed three times and it was pure good fortune that the ship was not hit.'

Eventually, at 1830 hrs that evening, the *Chobry* weighed anchor and steamed slowly down the fjord. Their escort, the destroyer *Wolverine* and the sloop, *Stork*, had gone ahead and were already out of sight over the horizon. They had started with a German obser-vation plane for company, but that too had now disappeared. As the evening grew chilly on deck the men went below to eat and sleep. One officer seemed rather pleased with the situation and said so. 'It's all very well,' replied Colonel Faulkner, 'but it only needs one bomb. It would go through this ship like a hot knife through butter.' He was also unhappy about the lack of any sort of cohesive plan for the attack. 'I have no information at all,' he told his officers. 'I do not know whether our landing will be opposed or not, but I think it will be pretty sticky, particularly if the German aircraft spot us.'

Just after midnight three Heinkel bombers attacked. The bombs were of large calibre and some, at least, were incendiary. As a result the ship went on fire almost as soon as the first bombs landed. It spread rapidly as the explosions had ruined the sprinkler system. The Battalion Fire Orderly endeavoured to get the hoses working, but the hydrants were empty. Worse still, the bombs had all landed near the senior officers' cabins. Colonel Faulkner was killed immediately, so were Major C.L.J. Bowen, Major R.A. Hacket-Pain, Lieutenant Freddie Lewin and Captains J.R. Durham Mathews and Brian O'Neill – the man who had complained about the delayed departure. According to one staff officer, 'The cabins collapsed like a pack of cards. The lights went out, the whole of the top decks amidships were immediately ablaze and very soon the main staircase seemed to have disappeared.'

The men were ordered on deck immediately. The different companies filed up in full kit and carrying their .303s and bren guns. They emerged to a scene of chaos. Aft was an inferno and there was a tremendous noise from the anti-aircraft guns, Very lights and rifle fire. The fire had divided the ship in two, with the result that the men came up on the forward side whereas the officers remained aft. 'Get on parade, face that way,' barked the familiar voice of Regimental Sergeant Major Stack. A solitary man cracked under the strain, broke rank and jumped overboard to almost certain death in the icy waters. The rest remained steadfast, standing to attention while the ship burned around them. The inferno was now threatening the ammunition stacked on deck, so lines were formed to dispatch the cases overboard. It was then discovered that the lifeboats forward could not be lowered as the power was cut off to the electrified winches. There was nothing for it but to remain calm and wait for their escort vessels to return. Realizing this, the Regimental Padre Cavanagh, began to recite the Rosary. And so with bared heads in the dark of night on a burning ship in the middle of the Arctic Circle, the men of the 1st joined in the familiar prayers they had learnt in schoolrooms and homes across the length and breadth of Ireland.

By the time *Stork* and *Wolverine* arrived, there was a score of men in the freezing water who had become isolated by the fire and forced overboard. *Stork* immediately launched a whaler to rescue them, while her guns kept the bombers busy. The lifeboats aft were at least working and were filling up with men, or already on the water.

Although the Heinkels still hovered at a safe height above the chaos, they stopped short of strafing the survivors and seemed more intent on photographing the event. Chivalry, it appeared, was still a part of modern warfare, at least among some sections of the Luftwaffe.

Several rescue parties were formed to search the ship for casualties and they brought the wounded up on deck. Four men were now reported missing and only the heroic actions of one of their comrades saved them from certain death. Guardsman 'Mushy' Callaghan, realizing the four were trapped in the hold, threw a rope over the side and swung from porthole to porthole until he found them. He then hauled them up the rope one by one and on to the deck. Witnesses' accounts of the sinking are full of admiration and respect for the Regiment. Commander Craske of the *Wolverine* said:

> I never before realized what the discipline of the Guards was. We got a gangway shipped forward and the men were ordered to file off on to us. There was no confusion, no hurry and no sign of haste or flurry. I knew there might be only a matter of minutes in which to get them off. I had four ropes fixed so as to hurry up the transfer. They continued to file steadily off in one line. I cursed and swore at them but they had orders to file, and they filed. I saw someone who seemed to me to be a young officer and in no measured terms I told him to get them off by all four ropes. In a second they conformed to this order by one of their own officers, still steadily and without fuss or confusion. Their conduct in the most trying circumstances, in the absence of senior officers, on a burning and sinking ship, open at any moment to a new attack, was as fine as, or finer than, the conduct in the old days of the soldiers on the *Birkenhead*. It may interest you to know that six hundred and ninety-four men filed on board the escort in sixteen minutes.

Lieutenant Compton, Royal Navy, who was in charge of one lifeboat had this to say: 'I must praise the courage and devotion to duty of the men of the Regiment who, in spite of finding themselves in an element which is certainly not their own, showed the greatest calm, without the slightest sign of panic.' In fact the Navy had some trouble convincing the troops to part with their kitbags and rifles, which most of the men had held on to through the whole crisis. The discipline of the Depot training had been deeply instilled and no mere naval calamity was about to shake it. The Admiralty report went thus:

> The battalion had been under frequent bombing attack all day, cooped up with the ship at anchor. Some three hundred men were collected on the forecastle with enemy planes overhead, the midship part of the vessel a raging furnace, fifty tons of ammunition in the hold and a rescuing destroyer alongside. Not a man moved until the order was given. The calm courage they showed can hardly, if ever, have been surpassed.

The Micks had done themselves proud to a man. As they turned to negotiate the seven-hour voyage back to Harstad, they left the blazing carcase of the *Chobry* to her own devices.

As the senior surviving officer, Captain David Gordon-Watson now took temporary command of the battalion. Many of the remaining officers were still semi-naked or in pyjamas, having been rudely awakened by the inferno. The sailors provided blankets and greatcoats and made plenty of hot coffee and cocoa. The *Wolverine* arrived back at Harstad first, having survived more enemy bombs on the journey. Those who were fit enough were ordered on full battalion parade while they waited for the *Stork*. When she arrived without Colonel Faulkner on board, they were devastated. It was only when the roll call was taken that it became clear that as well as their commanding officer, the battalion had lost five other senior officers and six Guardsmen. The Welsh Borderers had also run out of luck. Their ship had hit a rock and sunk, fortunately with little loss of life.

On 20 May, in the middle of yet another bombing raid, the Irish Guards left Harstad again, this time using a mixture of destroyers and puffers as Colonel Faulkner had suggested in the first instance. They reached their destination near Bodo at midnight and the next day they found the local headquarters. The situation further south was worsening with the Germans advancing and in complete control of the skies. The Scots Guards were putting up fierce resistance and slowing the enemy progress as best they could under the circumstances. It was decided to man the next line of defence with the Irish Guards. They made their stand at a place called Pothus on the banks of the River Saltelva some 10 miles south. They were now under the command of Captain H.C. McGildowny of No. 4 Company, who had rejoined them at Harstad. With the four companies of the Irish Guards, he had also at his disposal three companies of British Territorial volunteers, a troop of 25-pounders and a section each of Norwegian machine-gun and mortar units. No. 1 Company were posted across the river to guard access to the nearby bridge, while the remaining troops were camped in the surrounding woods. At 0100 hrs the sentries heard approaching footsteps. It turned out to be the 1st Battalion Scots Guards, footsore and exhausted from their efforts. There was little of the usual jocular banter exchanged between the battalions on this occasion, and the Micks could see they were in for some tough fighting ahead. After the Scots Guards had crossed, the bridge was blown up in error leaving the men of No. 1 Company dangerously exposed. They could hear the enemy firepower in the distance and then the dreaded Heinkels returned. They sprayed the woods with machine-gun fire while a group of dive-bombers also entered the fray. However the Guards had dug efficient trenches and were ably led by the redoubtable Regimental Sergeant Major Stack, who went on to win the Military Cross for his contribution to the campaign. Meanwhile No. 1 Company were still stranded and now also under heavy attack. It seemed only a matter of time before they would be overrun.

By late afternoon the Company Commander, Captain Eugster, ordered the withdrawal of his men across the now swollen river. The Guardsmen took the slings of their rifles and swiftly knotted them together. A volunteer then tied the 'rope' around his waist and made it to the other side with some difficulty. The Germans, realizing the post had been abandoned, now came up over the ridge and began firing on the men in the water. Still they crossed, with Captain Eugster standing in the centre helping each man, while Sergeant Major Thompson stayed on the bank to barrack anyone who hesitated.

The Germans now overran their previous position and were preparing for a large-scale attack on the woods. With this in mind and in the likelihood of being completely surrounded, Colonel Stockwell gave the order for a general withdrawal. Experience told him their situation was perilous. They would be retreating in the path of the advancing enemy without any transport and under constant threat from the air. Then, and literally out of the blue, their salvation appeared in the form of an ageing Gladiator plane which proceeded to shoot down three Heinkels and then went on to machine-gun the bewildered Germans on the ground. Under this unexpected cover the battalion pulled out and reached Rognan without further incident. Having waited for any stragglers they realized they had surprisingly few losses, given the odds. They owed a huge debt of gratitude to the pilot of the lone Gladiator.

After occupying a position on the Valnes peninsula for a few days the battalion returned by puffer to Harstad. Their stay was to be extremely short-lived however. The situation in Norway, overall, was worsening by the hour. Of more immediate concern to Churchill at this stage was the impending collapse of resistance in France and Belgium. In fact the decision to evacuate the Expeditionary Force had been taken a week earlier and the king of Norway had already been notified. He had sailed from Tromsø the previous day. At midnight on the same day as they had arrived back from their latest mission, battalion headquarters got the order: 'Destroyers *Firedrake* and *Fame* at quay. Five minutes to get aboard.' All superfluous equipment was immediately discarded and boarding commenced. They were ferried out by puffer to the *Lancastria*, the vessel that was to carry them back to Greenock, exactly two months to the day they left London. Once more Lady Luck was on their side, as a band of thick fog descended and seemed to follow them protectively across the North Sea. The aircraft carrier *Glorious* was not as fortunate and was sunk with all hands, just a few knots behind them.

While Christy and his fellow Guardsmen had returned with plenty of stories, an inescapable feeling of failure hung over the battalion. The campaign had not been a success and this was compounded by the fact that its failure was by no means down to the men of the 1st. It was also scant consolation when they heard of the capture of Narvik by a mixture of Norwegian, Polish and French fighters prior to leaving Norway. They had been inadequately armed for the fighting they took part in, while the indecision of the Expeditionary Forces HQ had cost much life. The steadfast courage and discipline of the men had seen them through and earned them valuable experience. Nonetheless, although the battalion would see fiercer fighting in Africa and Europe long after Christy had left, Norway would continue to leave a bad taste in the mouth for many years to come.

Chapter Three

'Layforce'

Much had changed in the two months since the Guards had been in Norway. Hitler had launched his blitzkrieg across the Low Countries and France only four weeks earlier, and had succeeded in completely surrounding the French and British forces. The Allies were forced to evacuate from Dunkirk and over several days they managed to get nearly 340,000 men back to Britain, despite having to leave all their heavy equipment behind. By the time the Guards arrived back at Wellington Barracks, a German invasion seemed inevitable. Britain stood alone and isolated, while mainland Europe was now firmly in the grip of the Nazis.

Despite the severity of the general situation, the battalion was given two weeks leave in early July to recover from the fiasco of Norway. Christy grabbed the opportunity with both hands, and took the boat back home. Those who met him at that time remember him having some burn scars on his face, no doubt as a result of the *Chobry* fire. While he would have minimized the danger he had been in to his mother, his appearance did nothing to abate her worry. By now Joe was in the Irish Army and the suggestion of Christy joining him was discussed at one stage. The question of whether this would be possible legally speaking, was never pursued further, however.

There was little point. Christy, not yet turned twenty, was adamant about where his future lay. He made light of their fussing and did his utmost to make his holiday a pleasant memory for all concerned. His tenacity at this point won out, and despite the prevalent anti-British feeling in the area, he held firm. It must be remembered that British soldiers on leave in the Free State at this time were advised to refrain from appearing in public, dressed in uniform. Whether Christy paid much attention to this warning is not known, but it certainly did little to curtail the fun. His few weeks' leave was remembered by neighbours and friends for the many singsongs and parties that took place around Cahernabruck during this brief sojourn. In any event, picking an argument with Christy would most likely not have been a wise move.

Arriving back in London, Christy discovered that while he was taking things easy his Commander in Chief had been very busy indeed. With the Germans poised for action just across the Channel, the severity of the situation demanded desperate action. Accordingly, Churchill called for ideas from within the War Office for the creation of an elite force to rival Hitler's Storm Troopers. Their primary task would be the defence of Britain in the event of an invasion. On 18 June he told his staff, 'We have always set our faces against this idea, but the Germans certainly gained in the last war by adopting it, and this time it has been a leading cause of their victory.'

As it happened, Lieutenant Colonel Dudley Clarke, thinking along the same lines, had recently been reading up on the very topic of elite forces. He had been greatly influenced by a book by Deneys Reitz about his experiences fighting the British in the Boer War. That book was called *Commando*. Clarke submitted a one-page plan for consideration and Churchill accepted it within forty-eight hours. As a veteran of the same war, Churchill recalled only too well the damage inflicted by a small band of well-trained farmers on superior British forces. He supported the idea completely, even down to the choice of name, 'The Commandos'. If the Germans attacked they would form small units of raiding parties and carry out a guerrilla war against them. In the event of the Germans deciding not to invade, the Commandos' training could be adapted to carry the war to mainland Europe.

The best troops from the five Special Service companies, survivors of the Norwegian campaign, would be bolstered by the formation of another four, to bring the full complement to about 5,000 men. The force was then to be formed into three battalions; the 7, 8 and 11 Commandos. The prime minister stressed the importance of recruiting men with initiative, who could think along unorthodox lines, as well as having the physical attributes for the unit. As Director of Combined Operations, responsibility for its organization fell to Sir Roger Keyes. He immediately appointed Captain Robert Laycock of the Royal Horse Guards, whom he knew of by reputation, as the new leader. Laycock was promoted to the rank of colonel and given specific charge of raising 8 Commando, which was to be formed mainly, though not exclusively, from the ranks of the Guards regiments. Churchill's own son, Randolph, volunteered immediately for 8 Commando (also known as the Guards' Commando), while Keyes' son, Geoffrey, joined the predominantly Scottish 11 Commando.

When Christy reported back for duty, he soon heard the rumours about the new unit. Word went around the ranks that volunteers were being sought for 'special service of an undefined hazardous nature.' This, of course, was music to the young man's ears. When he eventually got hold of an application form, he would have studied it with mounting enthusiasm. Applicants were required to have a high standard of physical fitness, with the ability to swim being mandatory. They also had to demonstrate endurance, initiative and self-reliance. The new unit was to be formed and trained in absolute secrecy. Although Christy had great respect for his parent Regiment, he had grown weary of the constant drilling and petty discipline that is part of all regular army life. He craved adventure, and this latest outfit looked like the best chance of providing it in the immediate future. He had little preconception of what he was joining, of course, as there was no existing model. Nevertheless, Christy applied and was accepted for training. On 14 August he was posted initially to Combermere Barracks, Windsor and then to Burnham-on-Crouch for initial training under the command of Captain Geoffrey Nicholson. Among the other officers there was Randolph Churchill.

With the Germans now only 20 miles away, there was little time to waste and the first recruits had already begun training in July at Inveraray and Largs in western Scotland. The training was more intense than in the Irish Guards, but they were all volunteers and there were no shirkers in the ranks. After a month at Windsor the men were sent to join up with the rest of the force in Scotland, and from Ayr they boarded a ferry to Arran, their home for the next six months of hard training. If Christy had a feeling of déjà vu, it was because of their close proximity to Greenock, from where he had sailed three months earlier. Commando troops received extra pay, and part of this was designed to cover accommodation when they were based in Britain. Instead of the usual barracks, the men were sent to lodge with local families on Arran, an arrangement that suited both parties generally speaking. But while the islanders soon adopted them into the community, there was precious little time for socializing.

The training was organized by Admiral Keyes and his team of instructors. The instructors had themselves already completed an intensive course at the Special Training Centre, Lochailort. The Commandos trained in physical fitness, orienteering, signalling, compass reading, survival, close quarter combat, weapons (including enemy arms), vehicle operation, demolition, amphibious and cliff assault and silent killing. They learned how to place explosive charges and how to get ashore from a landing craft in the middle of a storm. A special canoe section was set up using collapsibles called 'Folbots'. Weapons training was carried out with live ammunition to keep the senses alert. A Commando had to posses not only an abundance of stamina, he also had to be intelligent and able to think on his feet. There were no official assessments. If a man hadn't made the grade, the first he knew about it was when he received a Return to Unit travel voucher. There was no appeal procedure. None of this was fazing Christy, or Chris as his non-Irish pals preferred to call him. He celebrated both his twentieth birthday and Christmas on the island without much cheer, given that there were strict orders prohibiting alcohol.

However, New Year's Eve 1941 saw the Commandos celebrating in style. They enjoyed their first pint of beer since arriving on the island and they were well entitled to raise a toast. Not only was it Hogmanay, but they had also successfully completed their intensive training and were now primed for action. The only problem was that Hitler appeared to be having second thoughts. Operation 'Sealion', as his invasion plan was known, had inexplicably stalled. In one way, the Germans had become victims of their own success: victory in France had come so quickly that the military planners were caught on the hop. As a result, they were unable to mount an immediate assault. Britain would not escape completely, however. The Luftwaffe began their blitz of London and other cities in early September, inflicting huge civilian casualties.

It was now up to Churchill to decide on an alternative arena for his new elite force. With the threat of an invasion diminished, the Commandos were suddenly in a position to take the offensive. There was talk of Norway being the destination, which must have caused Christy to raise an eyebrow. Eventually it was decided that the Commandos would be used to best advantage in the Middle

East, given that Italy had finally joined the war on the side of the Axis. Egypt was of crucial importance to the British Empire not only for its oil resources, but also for the access it provided to the Mediterranean Sea and Indian Ocean via the Suez Canal. The British presence in Egypt, a mere 35,000 men, now found themselves sandwiched between the two Italian colonies of Libya and Abyssinia. They were outnumbered to an alarming degree, with the Italians having an army of 600,000 based in the two countries.

Churchill's first plan was to mount an attack on the island of Pantelleria, which lies halfway between Tunis and Sicily. Although it was small in size, the island was an Axis stronghold and was well defended. It was strategically important for control of the central Mediterranean and had an airfield complete with underground hangars for eighty warplanes. It was guarded by over eighty heavy gun emplacements and 11,000 Italian troops. Plans for an attack on the island, codenamed 'Workshop' were drawn up, only to be postponed later. On 29 January the operation was on again, and the three Commando units had begun embarkation – only to have it cancelled once more. This time the Luftwaffe had arrived in Italy and it was felt the assault fleet would be vulnerable to an attack from them. But the Middle East was still to be the destination and two days later the three battalions of Commandos boarded three converted assault ships, the *Glengyle*, the *Glenearn* and the *Glenroy*, and sailed down the Firth of Clyde bound for Cairo.

For security reasons, GHQ decided at this stage to designate them collectively as 'Layforce', after their leader. The last thing they wanted was for the enemy to get wind of an imminent assault by specialist forces. There was also some antipathy towards the name 'Commando', given its Boer War origins, though they were still known generally as the Commandos. Christy of course, was by now no stranger to the Firth of Clyde. He had taken the same route to Norway only nine months earlier, but as they headed for the open sea he would have been forgiven for hoping to himself, 'better luck this time'. While there were barely 1,500 men on board the three ships, Christy was now in exalted company. The list of ex-Sandhurst Officers among the troops read like a 'Who's Who' of British Society. As well as Randolph Churchill and Geoffrey Keyes, they numbered among them the novelist Evelyn Waugh and three Conservative MPs – the Second Earl of Jellicoe, Philip Dunne and Carol Mather.

Another officer on board with aristocratic lineage was the future founder of the SAS, David Stirling.

The voyage was long, and largely uneventful. They called at Freetown and Cape Town and did some drilling whenever the opportunity rose. This helped to prevent boredom and also ensured that the men were in peak condition when they eventually landed. This they did on 11 March at Geneifa, a short distance from Cairo. On disembarkation the reported All Rank strength of the battalions was as follows: 7 Commando, 577, including 36 officers; 8 Commando, 540, including 38 officers; 11 Commando, 533, including 35 officers. The Boat section had 12 Folbots and 19 men. Waiting to join the three Commandos were two new local units comprising 568 men. The men were immediately given strict instructions on the need for secrecy when they hit the local hot spots of Cairo, as the city was notorious for spies of every hue at the time. The Egyptian capital was legendary not only for practitioners of espionage, however – for sheer variety of sexual diversions, very few red-light districts in the world could hold a candle to Cairo at this time. Christy and his pals might have considered themselves wise in the ways of the world by now, but a stroll down the back streets of the notorious Wagh el-Birket must have been a jaw-dropping experience for all concerned. The commercial activity around Piccadilly may have been wondrous to a young country boy from the West of Ireland, but this was on another level completely. The 'Cairene tarts', as the local prostitutes were known, had been a constant headache to the British military during the First World War with venereal disease causing huge problems for the medics.

And little had changed this time around, despite the frequent warnings of staff HQ. The combination of sun, sand and a cosmopolitan atmosphere proved too much for the British 'Tommy' in most cases. The rumours of wild sexual activities, including houses that offered the spectacle of women copulating with a variety of animals, continued to lure the men. Accompanying this depravity was the usual sorry list of murders, rapes and robbery. To add to the confusion, there were soldiers from all corners of the world in Cairo – Australians, Greeks, Czechs and Poles mixed with the Tommies in the bars and brothels with inevitable consequences. A favourite watering hole among the British was the Sweet Melodies. All was fine and dandy during the day, but come ten o'clock at night there was usually pandemonium. With a Stella beer costing a mere two piastres and mixed with Arrack, the local spirit, the men could have a fine old time. The Military Police were barely managing to keep a lid on the situation. The officers' free time was spent a long way from this squalor. They lounged around private clubs such as the Jockey Club and the Continental, dressed in suede boots and carrying swagger sticks. They drank Tim Collinses and rye highballs and gambled recklessly. They also pursued the many European women who lived locally. The contrast with Christy's last experiences in the wilderness of the Norwegian fjords could not have been starker.

The Commandos were now officially assigned to General Sir Archibald Wavell, head of the Allied Middle East Command. Six months earlier the Italians had made a push to drive the Allies out of Egypt. But they only managed to cover 60 miles in four days before the Allies ground to a halt and decided to dig in where they stood. While they waited for fresh supplies, however, Wavell was boosted by the arrival of 31,000 fresh troops, as well as 275 tanks and 150 aircraft. The counter-attack began on 9 December and the Italians were soon in full-scale retreat, suffering high casualty rates and surrendering in their thousands. Hitler now decided to come to the aid of his newfound allies and on 6 February he appointed the charismatic General Erwin Rommel as Commander of the Axis troops in the Middle East. Rommel had already made a name for himself the previous year following the blitzkrieg across Europe. He would enhance his reputation in the African desert. Within weeks he had formed a new German troop, the 'Deutsches Afrika Korps'. From that point on, all the Allies' hard-earned gains were reversed. The British were pushed so far back that the Suez Canal was in danger of falling into German hands.

It was now imperative that General Wavell planned a response. The question was how to adapt the Commandos to this particular arena and how to make the best use of their particular training and skills. Tobruk turned out to be their first engagement. The Afrika Korps had surrounded the port in early April. Its capture was essential to the Germans as it provided the means of supplying their troops for the final push to the Suez. Defending Tobruk were 30,000 Allied troops, mostly Australian, who were now in dire need of reinforcements. A small battalion of 350 Commandos sailed from Alexandria to mount a surprise attack on the Germans. The trouble was nobody told the Germans it was a surprise. As half of the Commandos rowed towards the shore in their Folbots in the black of night, the Germans duped them by sending landing signals with their torches. As soon as the men landed they were mowed down. The big guns then turned on the two ships which had brought the men to Tobruk. This was to be remembered as one of the bloodiest and most suicidal missions of the entire war. No. 7 Commando was the next battalion to see action. On 20 April, along with the Royal Tank Regiment, they attacked the port of Bardia with some success. Although they inflicted minimum damage, Rommel diverted a large portion of the German Armoured Brigade from Sollum to defend the port, in the mistaken belief that a large-scale invasion was in progress.

The men had been specially trained for small-scale coastal assaults but it was becoming increasingly difficult to carry out such operations. Most of the infantry ships had been redeployed to Greece, where they were badly needed. German air power also meant that any transport slower than a destroyer became a sitting duck for the dreaded Stukkas. But it seemed the powers that be were determined to fragment the Commandos. On 26 April, 11 Commando were ordered to Cyprus to help defend the island. This was effectively the last straw for many of the men. They hadn't volunteered and gone through intensive training to end up on garrison duty. Nos 7 and 8 Commando were to remain at Alexandria for general service. They were soon to be in action. On 20 May the troops guarding Crete woke up to the rather unusual sight of thousands of German paratroopers dropping out of the clear blue sky. It was the largest ever use of paratroopers in an invasion up to that point, and the element of surprise proved to be very effective indeed. A ferocious battle soon ensued for control of this key island. Within eleven days the Germans had won out, despite fierce resistance from a combination of Allied troops and Greek Resistance fighters. Both sides had suffered heavy casualties, with the result that Hitler refrained from carrying out large-scale airborne operations in future.

For the Allies, the priority was now to evacuate the survivors as quickly as possible. With this in mind, 7 and 8 Commando along with the local battalion, under the command of Colonel Robert Laycock, were ordered to the island with instructions to fight a rearguard action covering the retreat. Finally, Christy and his comrades would have some of the action. However, their first attempt to get to the target was abandoned. They had left Alexandria in four destroyers only to run into worsening weather conditions. Their journey wasn't wasted however, as en route back to Egypt they rescued many survivors from the *Kashmir* and the *Kelly*. Both ships had been attacked and sunk, and among the lucky survivors that night was Louis Mountbatten, soon to become the new Commander of Combined Forces. As soon as they had dropped off the survivors, the Commandos returned to Crete, and this time they landed safely at Sphakia on the night of 26 May. They were continuously dive-bombed and strafed by Stukkas, but the men stood up well to these attacks. When asked his opinion of the attacks some time later, Evelyn Waugh commented: 'Like all things German, it was very efficient and went on much too long.' The Commandos soon took up positions along the only road that led southward to Sphakia and the coast. They then broke up into small units and waited for the Germans to arrive. From their secluded positions they ambushed the enemy, mostly at night. They engaged them in fierce hand-to-hand fighting, with many casualties accruing from bayonet wounds.

This was precisely the type of combat the men had trained for and it was now beginning to show results. Although the Commandos lacked artillery or mortars with which they could have created more devastation, the German advance had been halted for the present. Colonel Laycock and a detachment of 200 now joined the men of the 20th Heavy Anti-Aircraft Battery, who had been assigned to guard the Souda docks nearby. After one particularly heavy assault, Laycock decided to retreat under cover of darkness. However they were eventually cut off by superior German forces at a village called Babali Khani. Laycock and Waugh escaped by crashing through the enemy lines in a commandeered tank but most of the other men, including those from the 20th, were either killed or captured. Over the next four days the Commandos succeeded time after time in sending the Germans into retreat, allowing the bedraggled Allied troops to continue their trek to the beach and the safety of Egypt.

On 30 May, the Allied Commander in Crete, General Freyberg, was flown out by order to Cairo. Command then passed to General Edward Weston of the Royal Marines. When the Navy suspended evacuations later the same night, Weston was also ordered to evacuate via flying boat. He had been instructed to pass on overall command to Laycock, who was having none of it. 'I did not come to Crete to surrender to the Hun,' he replied, 'I believe I can be of greater service with my Commando Brigade than as a prisoner of war.' Having appointed Lieutenant Colonel Young in his place, Laycock left in the same plane as Weston, filled with remorse and pledging to return. By now some 20,000 men had been evacuated safely to rejoin the Eighth Army in Egypt and it was time for the Commandos to cut their losses. But by the time their turn came, there were very few seaworthy boats left. As a result, the fittest men were given priority, but many of the officers and men were left behind and subsequently taken prisoner. In all, the Commandos had lost 600 men – dead, wounded or missing – almost three-quarters of their strength. Christy was among the lucky number to make it back to Cairo.

The men had fought with great bravery and tenacity and had served the purpose of their mission well. However, 'Layforce' was now down to a single battalion. The problem for the top brass was how to replace the missing men. Resources were already well over-stretched and the proposition of training new recruits was not feasible. While they pondered this predicament, the situation in the Middle East in general was becoming more critical. As their influence in the region gained strength, pro-Nazi factions in Syria invited German 'technicians and advisors' into their country. Very soon the Luftwaffe were refuelling at Syrian airfields before going on to bomb the British oilfields in Iraq. The decision was taken to invade Syria immediately. Both Syria and Lebanon were occupied by an army of Vichy French, but the Allies looked on them as reluctant combatants and therefore poor opposition. Layforce was to spearhead the invasion by capturing a strategically important bridge over the Litani River in the Lebanon. The river was a natural barrier to any army heading northwards towards Syria, and if the Commandos could control it the Allies could make good progress.

On 7 June, the 11 Commando led by Lieutenant Colonel Richard Pedder left Cyprus on board the *Glengyle*. They had orders to take the Litani bridge and hold it for the first wave of the invasion, the Australian 21st Infantry Brigade. The Battalion strength was twenty-one officers and 456 other ranks. They had a considerable protection escort of three cruisers and eight destroyers, which turned out to be just as well. As they neared their objective they ran into a sizeable portion of the Vichy French Navy. After playing cat and mouse for several hours, the French grew weary and withdrew. However the landing was postponed for twenty-four hours as a result of the intrusion. The landing commenced at 0420 hrs the next morning, but the element of surprise had been lost due to the previous night's standoff. Enemy artillery and machine-gun fire killed many men even before they had left the beach. By now the Australians had arrived, just in time to see the French blowing up the bridge. The Commandos re-grouped and attacked the barracks. This time they prevailed and the Vichy forces were soon on the retreat. The Australians then crossed the Litani by way of temporary pontoons and continued their trek to Syria. The operation had been a success, but the Commandos had once again paid a high price – 123 men had been killed, including Lieutenant Colonel Pedder and several officers. One young officer who acquitted himself with distinction that day and lived to tell the tale, was an Irishman called Blair Mayne. Mayne would go on to play a pivotal role in Christy's future adventures, but for now his battalion was under pressure.

On 11 June, Lieutenant Colonel Keyes, the most senior surviving officer, went to Jerusalem to report to General Wilson, who expressed his satisfaction with the Commando operation. After three days recuperation the remnants of No. 11 went back to garrison duty on Cyprus. By now, General Claude Auchinleck was preparing to take over as Commander in Chief in the Middle East and the men were hoping for a change for the better. But the die had been well and truly cast by then. When Laycock met Keyes on 23 June he told him that disbandment was both inevitable and imminent. In fact, while 11 Commando continued with their garrison duty throughout July, Nos 7 and 8 were already preparing to disband, although a section of 8 Commando were still organizing raiding patrols against the Germans besieging Tobruk. The simple truth was that the Eighth Army had been suffering heavy casualties and was now short of men. The surviving members of Layforce numbered about 2,500 men and the top brass saw them as the ideal replacements. With morale at an all-time low, the Commandos were given the choice of going back to their old regiments. Although the men's frustration was palpable, very few took up the offer. They had tasted a different style of soldiering as Commandos and did not relish a return to the petty disciplines of ordinary army life.

One option open to Commandos was to become guerrilla warfare instructors in Burma. By now, the Japanese had been at war with China for some time and Churchill predicted they would soon declare war against the Allies. He had promised to assist the

Chinese in what would be a secret operation, given that Britain and Japan were not yet at war. The plan was to send out some ten officers and 100 men to a specially set-up camp with the grand title, 'The Bush School of Warfare'. There, along with a contingent of Australians, they were to drill the Chinese in the art of commando warfare. Several men also joined the Long Range Desert Group (LRDG) at this time. The LRDG was a unit of the Special Forces set up in Egypt after Italy declared war on the Allies. It was the brainchild of Major Ralph Bagnold, an expert in desert navigation, and was comprised mainly of soldiers from South Africa and New Zealand. The unit specialized in reconnaissance and intelligence gathering and was soon to play an important role in the early days of the SAS.

One group of officers were determined to carry on however, and set up a new group called the Middle East Commando. They were led by Lieutenant Colonel Geoffrey Keyes and Lieutenant Colonel Robert Laycock and were drawn almost exclusively from 11 Commando. The alternative left for those whose regiment was not currently serving in the Middle East was a return to the infantry depot base at Geneifa, and a life of boredom and stagnation. Unfortunately for him, Christy fell into this category. The next nine months were filled with drill duties, petty discipline and the odd bit of sport. Some of the drill sergeants resented the men for their 'Commando' tag, and did their best to make their lives difficult while they had the chance. The men were forced into the drudgery of barrack life, their only distraction being frequent visits to the dingy side streets of Cairo. Was this what all the gruelling training in Scotland had been about, they must have wondered. The surviving members of the elite of Britain's war machine were now reduced to garrison duties, far away from the action. There simply had to be a way out.

Chapter Four

A Legend is Born

'The boy Stirling is mad, quite, quite mad. However, in war there is often a place for mad people.'

Field Marshal Bernard Montgomery

Although he had been sent down from Cambridge for drinking and gambling, the ignominy of it all did little to dampen David Stirling's ambition. For a time he had studied art in Paris, but the prospect of becoming the first man to climb Everest fired his imagination, and that was the particular dream he was pursuing when he was rudely interrupted by Chamberlain's declaration of war in 1939. The privilege of being an officer helped Stirling to avoid the worst aspects of being garrisoned. He divided much of his time between lounging at his brother Bill's flat in Cairo and the various gentlemen's clubs in the city. However, any outward appearance of joviality masked the disillusionment he was feeling inside. His experiences as an officer of 8 Commando had been downright frustrating. While he had the utmost respect for Colonel Laycock, he felt there was too much interference from higher up the chain of command. This had resulted in missions going ahead when they should have been aborted, and vice versa.

Now as Layforce was disbanding, Stirling had got wind of some parachutes that were lying around in Port Said due to a shipping error. The concept of parachuting was still very new, but Stirling had been impressed by the impact the German paratroops had made in Crete. Having got permission from Laycock, Stirling and some fellow Commandos decided to try them out. They borrowed an old Vickers mail plane for the purpose and all landed safely, except Stirling. A faulty cord caused him to crash to the ground causing spinal damage. As a result, he was temporarily both blinded and paralysed from the waist down. It looked like the end of the war for the young officer, but he refused to give up. Recuperating in hospital, he now had ample time to consider what improvements could be made in the utilization of Special Forces in the future. He believed the deployment of Layforce had been akin to using a sledgehammer to crack a nut. The involvement of large ships and whole regiments of men attacking specific targets was both un-necessary and futile, he realized. Small units of four or five men could operate with better effect and at a fraction of the cost. They could exploit the element of surprise by approaching their target in small groups by land, air or sea, and whereas a whole Commando regiment could only achieve one or two landings per night, smaller units could infiltrate several locations at once if necessary.

'My whole concept was that we should be capable of reaching a target by air, sea or land, and we could arrive without making any demands on expensive equipment,' he recalled, many years later. His proposition also had several controversial suggestions, or what he called 'first principles'. These first principles are still the bedrock of today's SAS. He believed the new unit had to be regarded as a totally new type of force, and above all it had to be independent. He wanted to develop new methods and techniques, free from the interference of Middle East headquarters, with the new unit having its own special status. But Stirling had a problem. The very people he needed to go through, in order to have his proposition accepted, were busy determining a way to get rid of him. They'd had their eye on Stirling for some time and suspected his injuries were self-inflicted. In fact they had set up an inquiry to look into his antics by this stage, and there was even talk of a court martial.

An even bigger obstacle to progress was the reluctance of those in command to accept any kind of new thinking. 'There was an enor-mous residue of staff officers from the First World War who didn't fight, who set the spirit of the administration. And it was ludi-crously swollen ... and wholly obstructive to anything that looked like a new idea,' Stirling recalled. Major Ralph Bagnold had en-countered these same obstacles when he introduced the concept of the LRDG the previous year, and without the personal backing of Churchill it seems unlikely that Layforce would ever have come into existence. He decided to emphasize the use of parachutes, as he felt it would be a good means of selling his idea to the top brass. A new unit with its own unique transportation methods might have a better chance, he reasoned. By now General Auchinleck had replaced Wavell as Commander in Chief, and Stirling hoped the new man might be more receptive to his idea, if he could only get it across. Having checked himself out of hospital and still on crutches, he was determined to take his plan to the very top. Without an official pass, he opted to slip the sentries at HQ by scaling the fence. The sight of the six-foot-five Stirling on crutches, dragging himself over the wire must have unnerved the guards, but he made it. By pure good fortune he eventually arrived at the door of Major General Ritchie and, with the sentries in hot pursuit, he managed to knock and enter in the nick of time.

Three days later Stirling was back at HQ and this time he not only had a pass, but an appointment with General Auchinleck himself. The new chief immediately promoted Stirling to the rank of captain and gave him the go-ahead to recruit six officers and sixty other ranks. Stirling soon demonstrated his pragmatic nature when deciding on a name for his new outfit. Brigadier Dudley Clarke was in charge of deception tactics in Egypt, and had been dropping hundreds of dummy parachutes near the Italian prisoner of war camps. The hope was that word would eventually reach Rommel that the Allies were training a new air-borne division. Stirling adopted the name Clarke had given his phantom unit in the hope of causing more confusion for the Germans, but also because he admired Clarke and felt he could be influential in any future spats with HQ. The full title of the new unit was 'L Detachment, Special Air Service Brigade' on the insistence of Clarke, who coincidentally had also picked the name, 'Commandos'. As his second-in-command, Stirling picked the officer who had first tipped him off about the 'mislaid' parachutes they had used in their first jump, Lieutenant Jock Lewes. Lewes's personality could not have been more different from that of his new boss. Australian by birth, he was every bit as aristocratic as Stirling and was an ex-president of Oxford University's rowing club. But he was a puritan by nature and did not share Stirling's liking for socializing or gambling. Among the other officers picked was a Dubliner called Eoin McGonigal, who in turn suggested his friend and fellow officer, Blair 'Paddy' Mayne. The two men had become firm pals while serving in the Royal Ulster Rifles and had joined the 11 Commando together. Mayne had a ferocious temper and had got into trouble for striking his superior, Geoffrey Keyes, after Keyes disrupted a chess game between Mayne and McGonigal. While it is generally believed that court martial charges were pending for this offence, there is little evidence to back it up, although Mayne was in jail when Stirling came to his rescue. What is certain though, is that Stirling impressed upon Mayne that there could not be a recurrence of the incident: 'I had to tell him that this superior officer was not for hitting,' he remembered. Mayne gave his new boss his word, and kept it. Along with Mayne and McGonigal, there were several other Irish names among the ranks of the original sixty-six SAS men. Names like Joe Duffy, Pat Reilly and Cornelius McGinn who was quickly nicknamed 'Maggie', his Christian name being too much of a mouthful for most. Pat Reilly was an Irish American who had lied about his nationality in order to fight. This is how he remembered his recruitment into the regiment:

> One day in Tobruk, I went down to collect some rations and heard what you might term idle conversation about do-or-die boys being formed in Egypt, and I came back and had a quiet word with Jock [Lewes], and said, 'I gather it's a do-or-die outfit that you people are forming.' All he said to me was, 'What? Getting worried?' And I said, 'No, we'll stop here as long as you want to stop.'

Why the name Chris O'Dowd did not appear at this stage in the unit's formation is not clear. There is some evidence that he may have been home on leave at this time, and therefore was absent when Stirling visited Geneifa as part of his recruitment drive. However, given the lack of documentary evidence it seems logical to assume that he simply wasn't chosen. Although they were both in the same Commando, officers would have had little contact with soldiers who were not directly under their command and it is possible the two young men had not met at this point. Whatever the reason, Christy was left kicking his heels back at the barracks with the bulk of his fellow Guardsmen.

While he had been overlooked initially, Christy's time would come soon enough. Meanwhile, Stirling was now a man in a hurry. The men were told to make their way to a base camp at Kabrit. It was an inhospitable spot, 90 miles east of Cairo on the edge of the Great Bitter Lake. When they arrived at the rendezvous, they were surprised to find the place deserted apart from the usual swarms of flies and a small board stuck in the ground with the words, 'L Detachment SAS' scrawled across it. It wasn't long before some wag added the words, 'Stirling's Rest Camp' underneath. As it turned out Stirling was still being obstructed in certain quarters, despite having the blessing of the Commander in Chief. When he eventually turned up it was to tell the men that their first mission was to steal a base camp. This was to be only the first of many examples of his incredible ability to skirt around formalities, when the need arose. His new recruits warmed to their task, and under cover of darkness they drove up to a New Zealand infantry camp, which happened to be more or less empty. They stole the lot including a piano, and by the morning they had one of the best base camps in the area (although the piano was later returned as a peace offering to the understandably irate Kiwis). Among the men Stirling had picked was a sharp Londoner called Kaufman. He couldn't take the training so he was appointed canteen manager. It was a job he was more suited to, though not necessarily for his cooking skills. His speciality was to drive around the other camps and engage the quartermaster of the stores in conversation, while his accomplices filled the truck with provisions. He even managed to pinch a load of bricks from the Air Force and ordered some prisoners of war he had rounded up to build a canteen. The men relied on him to keep body and soul together in those early months in the face of HQ neglect.

Then it was down to some serious training and planning. Although the men were already highly trained, they were told that if they didn't come up to scratch they were out. Route marches of 20 miles were the norm, while a lot of effort was put into initiative and memory tests. The men also became experts in desert navigation and survival skills. In fact the training regime that Lewes improvised back then still forms the foundation of that used by the present day SAS. When it came to parachuting however, they were all novices. Stirling had put in a request for instructors to be sent from England, but was promptly refused. This was soon to have fatal consequences for two of the 'Originals'. Undaunted by the latest knockback, Stirling got hold of some parachutes and Lewes had scaffolding erected for jump training. They also practised jumping from lorries while travelling at up to 40 miles per hour. Lewes was a born leader and would not ask the men to do anything he was not himself prepared to try. The men would often see the oil lamp in his tent burning on deep into the night, while he drew up plans for the latest training technique for the following morning. While the training was tough, its rigours were somewhat offset by the relaxed attitude to discipline. Officers were on first name terms with their men and petty army rules such as the constant saluting of superior officers were ignored. Shining buttons and polishing boots were no longer the be all and end all, which suited the band of vagabonds and misfits that Stirling had mobilized down to the ground. They appreciated the common sense approach shown by their Commanding Officer, and respected him all the more for it. It wasn't that discipline was slack, far from it. Stirling himself put it this way: 'We had far sterner discipline than any Brigade of Guards regiment, but it was of a different nature, a different type, a much more exacting type of discipline.'

The men also looked up to Lewes, despite his serious nature. They soon realized that their second-in-command was both a perfectionist and a deep thinker. Reg Seekings, who had joined from 7 Commando expressed it thus: 'People like David Stirling and Paddy Mayne [later], they gave us the opportunity to share in it properly. Not just the business of an officer directing operations and pulling his poor little ignorant privates along. You were treated as one of a team, and this made a big difference. That's what everybody was after.' In fact the two leaders complemented each other perfectly. While Stirling spent a lot of time in Cairo cajoling equipment and favours wherever he could, Lewes dealt with the more practical elements such as training and planning. Stirling's plan involved parachuting hundreds of miles behind enemy lines to attack airstrips and ports. In order to inflict maximum damage, Lewes realized they needed a new type of hand-bomb. It had to be small enough to carry in large quantities and have the ability to ignite and explode simultaneously. Dismissing the pessimism of the RAF engineers, Lewes began his own experiments. After several weeks he came up with the now famous 'Lewes bomb', a weapon that was to prove invaluable to the Regiment's future success. It was designed to destroy plane wings and ignite the fuel they carried, and consisted of 1lb of plastic explosive rolled in a mixture of thermite and old engine oil. Time pencils and detonators could be carried separately and attached just before use.

Eventually, Jock Lewes felt the men were ready for their first jump. Stirling acquired some beat-up pre-war Bristol Bombays for the purpose, and the exercise was to be carried out in two lifts.

Disaster struck soon after the first plane took off. As the rest of the men watched it approach the drop zone at around 900 feet, they noticed something fall from the plane amongst all the parachutes. When the plane landed they learned that two men, Joe Duffy and Ken Warburton, had fallen to their deaths. The two were best pals. Jock Lewes inspected the unopened chutes immediately and found that as the men had jumped, the pressure had caused the parachute clip to buckle, which in turn disengaged the static line ring from the rail. It later emerged that the RAF were aware of this problem but had not thought to warn Stirling. It was the evening of 16 October and the new regiment had suffered its first casualties. Lewes later spoke to the men and explained what had happened. He was adamant that the rest of the men would jump in the morning, once the fault had been fixed. He then offered them the chance to opt out and be RTU (Returned To Unit) – not one man accepted. The next day the jump was completed without a hitch.

Stirling was anxious to legitimize his unit as a proper regiment as soon as possible, and with this in mind he ran a competition among the men to pick a motto and emblem for his fledgling outfit. The original motto chosen was 'Descend to Defend', but Stirling himself finally decided on the now famous, 'Who Dares Wins'. The original emblem of the winged Excalibur was designed by Sergeant Bob Tait and lives on to this day. Tait had been awarded the Military Medal while with the 11 Commando and would go on to win another with his new regiment. Stirling then had the badges made in Cairo and the men began wearing them immediately. This infuriated HQ who had not authorized any emblem. His next move was even more audacious and had the effect of putting the noses of the top brass even more out of joint. General Auchinlech paid the unit a visit some weeks later and as he inspected the line of men, Stirling was at his side. As the General was coming up to the salute, Stirling turned to him and Auchinleck saluted his badge. This one act legitimized the regiment forever according to Army custom. Although he soon realized he had been duped, the General saw the funny side of it and later complimented Stirling on his initiative.

And initiative was to prove a decisive factor in the Regiment's first operation. The island of Malta was central to both sides' plans for an upcoming offensive. The Allies planned to push back the enemy lines and retake Tobruk. By capturing the airfields of Gazala and Timimi, they would also be able to supply Malta with airlifts.

From Malta, the RAF could eventually attack Sicily and the Italian mainland. Rommel, on the other hand, was preparing his own attack. If he succeeded in driving the Allies further east, he could prevent them from supplying the island, which was being used as a base for attacking German convoys. More importantly, it would clear the way for the convoys to reach North Africa, itself. The timing for the Allied offensive, Operation 'Crusader', was scheduled for 17–18 November. The SAS would play a key role in the attack. Their plan was to parachute into the airfields of Gazala and Timimi at midnight on the 17th, and to inflict the maximum damage. By neutralizing the superior enemy air power, they would give the main offensive a realistic chance of success the next day. They would then trek across the Great Sand Sea desert before rendezvousing with the LRDG, who would carry them back to base. L Detachment was to be divided into three units for the purpose of the operation. Troop 1 led by David Stirling, Troop 2 led by Jock Lewes and Troop 3 led by Blair 'Paddy' Mayne. Meanwhile, Major General Laycock had just returned to Egypt after pleading with Churchill to maintain a Commando presence in the region. Despite the usual baulking by HQ, he was authorized to lead a raid on Beda Littoria, where it was believed Rommel had his quarters. Laycock was to arrive at the Libyan coast via submarine, also at midnight, with about fifty men from the remnants of 11 Commando. Their mission was to kill or capture the German general. The outcome of these two missions would have serious ramifications for the future of the two units involved. Laycock was hoping to prove the value of his experienced Commandos, while Stirling was determined to establish the credentials of his more maverick SAS.

Early on 16 November 1941, L detachment SAS took off on their first mission. They had learned of the attack the previous day and had prepared themselves thoroughly. Five hours later they landed at their departure point, Bagoush airfield, some 300 miles west of Kabrit. For the next few hours the RAF indulged them with a scrumptious meal and a few drinks, while outside a storm began to brew. With a force nine wind blowing, Stirling was given the option of aborting the mission by MEHQ. He gathered the men around him and told them the latest. He was determined to carry on, but offered anyone the chance to opt out without loss of face. There were no takers. Like their Commanding Officer, the men had been through enough cancellations to last a lifetime, from their days in the

Commandos. At 0630 hrs they fitted their parachutes and boarded three Bristol Bombay transport planes. The top speed of a Bombay was 150 miles per hour, a fact which gave rise to the joke that you could open the door of one, take a toilet break, catch up to it again and climb back in. The pilots were forced to drop altitude to try and get some bearings, but still had difficulty trying to make out the coastline. As well as the gale, they also had a sandstorm and torrential rain to contend with. They suggested returning to base, but the offers were once more refused.

As the planes approached their targets they were immediately picked out by searchlights and the flak soon followed. Under fire and miles off course, the men jumped into the worst storm the region had seen for thirty years. As they landed on solid ground the parachutes dragged them over the rocks and scrub, causing multiple injuries. Some were killed outright by the impact, including Eoin McGonigal. Others had injuries which rendered them immobile. To compound things further, the Lewes bombs that were dropped separately were now missing. Given the dire circumstances, they had no choice but to abort the mission and try to make good their escape. Those who were too badly injured to carry on were left where they lay, with just a water bottle and a pistol to face the enemy and the elements. Although they had all been warned of the likelihood of such a predicament, it was understandably hard for the able-bodied men to walk away. They had close bonds with their injured comrades, and some were loyal friends.

The three sections, now separated and scattered to the four winds, took their bearings and headed towards the desert and their pick-up point. The Great Sand Sea is an inhospitable place at the best of times, but they were now experiencing the heaviest downpours ever seen in terrain where it hadn't rained for twenty years. The men were wading knee-deep in floods for much of the time, stopping occasionally at a dry spot for some sleep. When the storm abated, it was immediately replaced by scorching desert sun. After three days Jock Lewes's group made it to the rendezvous. Hours later Paddy Mayne's group showed up, while David Stirling and the one other survivor from his section made it back the next day. They knew for sure that six men had died and after a search for any stragglers, they listed a further thirty-four men as missing. Many of those listed would never be heard of again. Of the sixty-two men who set out, only twenty-two had returned. Many of the remaining SAS men feared the worst for the future of their regiment, but not Stirling. He was already making fresh plans with David Lloyd-Owen, who was in command of the LRDG unit. It was the airborne element of the operation that had caused the grief, they both realized. But if the LRDG could spirit them from a target, they could also get them there just as easily. When they arrived at the LRDG base Stirling put his idea to their CO, Colonel Guy Prendergast, who promptly accepted it. Stirling also realized that reporting back to MEHQ would spell disaster. They would be only too keen to disband his rabble of men. Instead he instructed them to return to Kabrit and muster as much supplies as they could manage. Meanwhile, he would report to Eighth Army HQ, paint a better picture of things, and hope for a stay of execution. He would return within a week. As luck would have it, the man he reported to was his old friend, General Ritchie. The offensive had not gone well and General Cunningham had taken the rap for it – and was replaced by Ritchie. After putting a gloss on events, Stirling was told to carry on.

He also learned that the Commando raid on Rommel's quarters had been a disaster. As it turned out the 'Desert Fox' was not in his lair (it transpired later that he was in Rome at the time). Of the entire force of fifty-four, only Laycock and Sergeant Jack Terry made it back to British lines. They arrived just in time for Christmas after having spent forty-one days trekking through the Libyan desert. The others had been either killed or captured including Colonel Keyes, son of the Commander of Layforce, who was fatally shot in the early stages of the raid. He was later awarded the Victoria Cross. To cap it all, the mission had been a waste both of time and good men. The area that they attacked was in fact a supply depot and had never been home to Rommel. Bad intelligence had been their undoing, and it spelled the end of any likelihood of a Commando regiment being re-established. Brigadier John Marriot was an old friend of Stirling's and after the latter had bent his ear about his unit's predicament, Marriot suggested a move to Jalo oasis, which was well ahead of the Allied lines. Brigadier Denys Reid had captured the post and was using it to launch forays against the enemy. It lay northwest of the Great Sand Sea, about 400 miles from Benghazi, and was ideally situated for Stirling's purposes. The fact that the LRDG were already operating out of there was an added bonus. Reid was informed of the idea and welcomed it wholeheartedly. All of this was done unofficially and without the knowledge of MEHQ. It went against all rules and regulations, but as far as Cairo knew, L Detachment SAS had disappeared off the face of the earth, and no one seemed particularly bothered.

Stirling then sent word to his twenty-one survivors to meet him at their new base. Reid's plan was to push towards the coast to take Benghazi, and Stirling determined to prepare the way. On the night of 14 December, Stirling and Mayne gathered a party to attack Sirte airfield. At the last moment they decided to split up, Stirling aiming for Sirte, with Mayne opting to attack Tamit airfield, close by. Meanwhile Jock Lewes and his men headed for Aghila airfield on the same night. Stirling found his target heavily defended and was forced to cancel. Lewes discovered his airfield was deserted, although the group managed to shoot up an Italian roadhouse on their way back. However, Mayne had better luck, accounting for twenty-four enemy planes. While the planes burned, they attacked the pilots' mess with machine-guns and grenades. Not to be out-done, Lieutenant Bill Fraser and his group destroyed thirty-seven planes in an attack on Agedabia one week later. This proved to be a real feather in the cap for Fraser, who felt he had a lot to prove. He had joined the 11 Commando from the Gordon Highlanders and had been the last officer to be picked by Stirling. Although soldiering was in his blood, he looked puny at the best of times. He mixed little with his fellow officers and when he did enter the officers' mess for a drink he was often ribbed, especially by Mayne.

These initial raids proved once and for all that Stirling's theory was sound. But far from dwelling on their successes, the men spent the whole of Christmas, including Christmas Day, being transported by the LRDG to and from targets deep behind the lines. They were sometimes dropped 20 or 30 miles from an airfield, and would then trek the rest of the way to their target and back again. Occasionally they would hole up somewhere for days, watching enemy move-ments and waiting for the right moment to strike. They survived on rations of bully beef, sardines, hard-tack biscuits and water. Mayne and his group returned to Tamit and destroyed another twenty-seven aircraft, but the unit was dealt a tough blow when Jock Lewes was killed, after his party was strafed by enemy planes returning from a raid. In only a couple of weeks twenty-one SAS men had destroyed over 100 enemy aircraft, something the RAF had not managed over several months. L Detachment had made an impression on the enemy behind the lines; it was now time to face 'the enemy within'. Stirling first moved the men back to their old base at Kabrit and then presented himself at MEHQ. It turned out they had all been mystified as to who was attacking the enemy airfields, until the Eighth Army HQ had put them wise. Without hesitation, General Auchinleck gave him permission to recruit six officers and thirty to forty men. Not only that, but 'The Auk', as he was affectionately known, promoted him to Major, with Mayne becoming a Captain. It was at this time also that Stirling learned of the Americans entering the war. Things were looking up for the gambling major. The new rank gave him the clout he so badly needed. The 'fossilized shits' who had given him so much grief in the past, could now do little to frustrate the future. Stirling had dared. He had dared desperately, and won.

Chapter Five

Chris Gets His Wings

'In the SAS you were treated as men; in the rest of the army you
did what the sergeant said or what the lieutenant said, but in
the SAS ... you got your say.'

Jimmy Storie, SAS Original

The new recruiting drive resulted in the SAS now taking on a more
cosmopolitan dimension. From Alexandria, Stirling recruited fifty
Free French parachutists, having driven to Beirut to get General
de Gaulle's permission. To add to the mix, some members of the
ancient Greek Sacred Squadron also joined up. But there were still
some good men languishing in various barracks around the Middle
East and over the next six months Sergeants Johnny Rose and Bob
Liley were given the task of picking them out. Meanwhile Stirling,
having left Blair Mayne in charge of training at Kabrit, returned to
Jalo with a dozen men, suitably refreshed and determined to cause
more havoc for Rommel. They attacked the port of Bouerat, destroying key installations without suffering any casualties, despite
having to fight off an Italian ambush.

When they returned to Jalo, however, it was practically deserted.
They were disappointed to learn from the remaining LRDG men
that Rommel had launched a counter-offensive and had succeeded
in retaking most of Cyrenaica in the process. With a massive enemy
assault imminent the SAS headed back to Kabrit, where Stirling
encountered another problem. His second-in-command was not a
happy camper, and told his commander in no uncertain terms. Blair
Mayne was not cut out for training men. He was not enamoured
with his role as a glorified sergeant major and demanded to see
action. Stirling took his point; Mayne had, after all, led the most

55

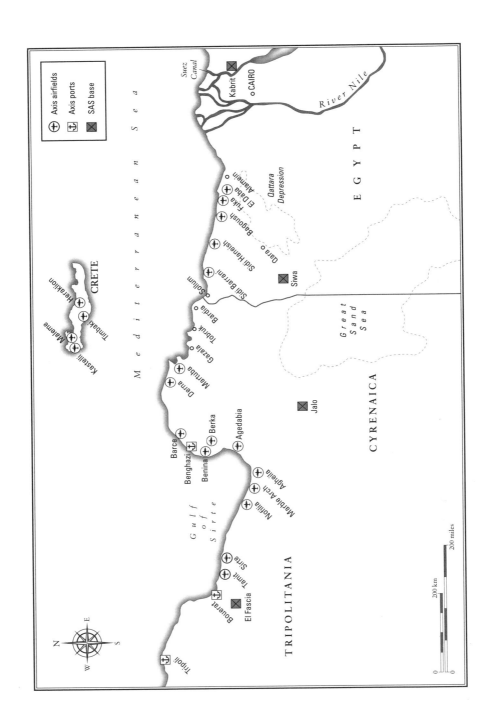

Legend:
⊕ Axis airfields
⊞ Axis ports
⊠ SAS base

CRETE
Maleme
Kasteli
Timbaki
Heraklion

Mediterranean Sea

Suez Canal
Kabrit
CAIRO
River Nile

EGYPT

Alamein
El Daba
Fuka
Bagoush
Sidi Haneish
Qara
Qattara Depression

Sidi Barrani
Sollum
Bardia
Tobruk
Gazala
Martuba
Derma
Siwa

Great Sand Sea

Barce
Benghazi
Benina
Berka
Agedabia
Aghelia
Marble Arch
Nofilia
Jalo

CYRENAICA

Gulf of Sirte

Sirte
Tamit
Bouerat
El Fascia

TRIPOLITANIA

Tripoli

N
E
W
S

200 km
200 miles

successful raids to date. He relieved him of training duties, appointing the newly promoted Pat Reilly in his place. This was to be the first and last time that these unique characters were to cross swords. From that day forward they remained the best of friends and confidants.

Meanwhile, back at HQ, General Auchinleck decided to take command of the Eighth Army himself, and was now planning to halt Rommel in his tracks. It was essential that the SAS now planned their operations to complement what the High Command had in store for the 'Desert Fox'. So while HQ were preparing the counter-attack, the obvious target area for Stirling's men was the port of Benghazi and the airstrips surrounding it. Benghazi was an intrinsic part of the German supply lines and their bombers used it as a base from which to attack Allied convoys bound for Malta. The first SAS raid took place in mid-March and resulted in sixteen planes being destroyed. This was also the first time Stirling used his 'Blitz Buggy' – a 25 hp Ford utility car he had commandeered from the enemy. It was painted olive grey to look like a German staff car and had the proper insignia on the sides. The windows and roof were removed and a twin Vickers K machine gun was fixed to the rear, with a single Vickers K at the front. Again, while they managed to kill several dozen Germans, the unit suffered only a few casualties. Stirling was not satisfied however, and vowed to return.

There was a communal raising of eyebrows among the men one morning in April, when a slightly portly officer arrived at the camp, apparently well aware of his own importance. It turned out to be none other than Major Randolph Churchill, son of the PM. He had already made a somewhat dubious impression on his fellow soldiers by gambling and drinking the equivalent of three months' salary, during the voyage to Egypt with Layforce. He was certainly not SAS material and the new posting was obviously his father's idea. Since the disbandment of Layforce, he had been more suitably employed at MEHQ's propaganda department. His marriage was now on the rocks, but if a spell with L Detachment was meant to sort him out, it failed miserably. He had whisky delivered to his tent every night and was constantly drunk. On one occasion he was found unconscious, in the nude, lying outside his tent in the midday sun. In a letter to his mother, Stirling wrote that Churchill's parachute training had been 'tremendously entertaining'. He continued that the PM's son had lost one and a half stone since joining, but was still 'damn fat'. The other men tolerated him, just. He was, in one veteran's opinion, a 'big, blustering, fat, useless no-good.'

Between raids, Sergeants Rose and Lilley were continuing with the recruitment drive. They arrived back from Geneifa one sunny day in May with the latest bunch of hopefuls, and among the excited group who alighted from the truck was young Christy O'Dowd. Their enthusiasm was understandable, having survived the monotony of barrack life for over half a year. Before leaving Geneifa, they had undergone an interview to determine their suitability. They would have been made aware that this was a 'do-or-die' outfit engaged in dangerous missions hundreds of miles behind enemy lines, but they were mostly ex-Commandos and relished the idea of seeing action again. They would also have heard of their future regiment's exploits through everyday barrack gossip. To Chris, it must have felt like the final day at Gortjordan School before the summer holidays. He was, at just twenty-one years of age, about to become one of the youngest members of L Detachment SAS. There was, of course, the small matter of a gruelling training course to come. Those who couldn't cut the mustard would be RTU'd, considered by many to be a fate worse than death itself.

Kabrit was a headland on the shores of the Bitter Lake, near its junction with the Suez Canal. The camp now consisted of a collection of sandbagged tents, one of which was a canteen, containing the famous stolen piano. However most of the SAS men, by now numbering about a hundred, spent their leisure time in the mess of HMS *Saunders*, the naval camp next door. Behind the cluster of tents stood the platforms and trolleys constructed for parachute training, and a large boxing ring. Further back towards the lakeshore were two areas reserved for signal and explosives training. The men slept five or six to a tent, and after a day's training sleep came easily. One of the first things a new recruit noticed about the camp was the quietness. This was due to the absence of the usual bawling sergeant majors. There was no need to salute an officer every time you passed one and after you had met you usually called him by his Christian name. At meal times, on the cook's shout of 'come and get it', the men queued up together regardless of rank. This sense of informality could lead a volunteer into a false sense of security, however. Jeff DuVivier, an original from day one, was one of the instructors at this time. 'I suppose I did have a lot of say in who passed and who failed. We watched them very carefully to see how they behaved during training. You sort of knew instinctively who was going to make it and who wasn't. It was a personality thing.'

While it must be left to conjecture as to which officer Christy met first after his arrival, he must have been impressed, whether it was the sophisticated David Stirling, the true gentleman who had the knack of instilling a man with enough confidence to do anything he asked of him, or the somewhat eccentric Bill Fraser. Lieutenant (later to become Major) Fraser looked nothing like an SAS man. He was lightweight in comparison to most of the rest, with protruding ears and melancholy eyes. He kept to himself a lot, preferring the company of his beloved dachshund, Withers. Fraser usually wore kilts while Withers looked resplendent in a naval coatee. Perhaps Christy first ran into his fellow countryman, Blair 'Paddy' Mayne here. Mayne was usually to be found in the mess of an evening, propped on a parachute cylinder (they made ideal bar stools), his distinctive County Down accent discernible through the din. A qualified solicitor, he had been an outstanding lock forward for the Irish rugby team and had toured South Africa with the British and Irish Lions. He had also been the Irish University heavyweight boxing champion in his time, and had only recently ripped out the cockpit of a German Stukka with his bare hands, after running out of Lewes bombs.

Malcolm James Pleydell, who joined the regiment as a medical officer at the same time as Chris, writes of Mayne in his book (under the pen name Malcolm James), *Born of the Desert*:

> Paddy was a bit different from the others – this sort of fighting was in his blood; he thrived on it. There was no give or take about his method of warfare, and he was out to kill when the opportunity presented itself. There was no question of sparing an enemy – this was war, and war meant killing. No quarter was asked and none was given. Nor can I remember having heard him complain about the enemy's methods of warfare in the desert, for to him there were no rules. Once or twice I heard him question the value of the Red Cross, remarking that a soldier who was going to be built up to fight again should, in his opinion, be a perfectly legitimate target. He observed the rules and the Red Cross, mind you, but his theory was that the days of *noblesse oblige* and the Knights of King Arthur stuff had drawn to a close, and that now it was all or nothing. Neither did

59

you hear him complain when his friends were killed; but I always felt, although he would say nothing other than giving an expression of sorrow, that a friend's death meant so many enemy lives in a form of personal revenge, a wiping off of the debt as it were.

Mayne had a violent temper, especially when drinking and did not suffer fools gladly. He was prone to settle any perceived wrong by offering the offender a few rounds in the camp boxing ring, but there were few takers. Nevertheless, Mayne was not a bully nor was he reckless in the heat of battle. He instilled great loyalty amongst his men and they trusted him implicitly as a leader. His family were prominent Presbyterian business people from Newtownards, and according to some early accounts of his character, he disliked Catholics and southern Irish in general. However, even the most cursory look at the facts shows that he didn't have a sectarian bone in his body. He had been born before the country was partitioned and many of his pals from the Irish rugby team were from the south. Irish rugby teams have always ignored the border, whereas Association Football sides have always been separate. It is unlikely that Chris would have heard of Mayne's rugby prowess prior to the SAS however, given that Gaelic football was the prominent sport in the west of Ireland. Mayne was proud to be Irish and liked nothing more after a few jars than to belt out 'The Mountains of Mourne' or 'Come Back, Paddy Reilly' at the top of his somewhat unmelodic voice.

The two men would share many a singsong in the future, but for now, for Christy, there was the serious matter of getting in shape and gaining his wings to attend to. As soon as reveille was blown in the morning the camp became a hive of activity. While the Regiment had not used parachutes on an operation since the first disastrous raid, Stirling held true to his early principles; they must still have the capability to arrive at their target by land, air, or sea. By now, attitudes at HQ were changing for the better, and the Regiment had been given two RAF parachute instructors, Peter Warr and Bernard Schott. The men jumped off 12-foot towers and trolleys set in rail tracks. They practised rolling in various directions depending on the wind, before ever attempting a sky jump. Sprains and broken bones were commonplace, but at least the camp now had proper medical facilities. Whatever the pain and effort, being awarded your parachute wings was a source of great pride amongst the new recruits. While some men seemed to handle the training better than others, parachuting was the great leveller. The concept was still relatively new, and most would admit to having second thoughts about taking the literal leap of faith. Anyone refusing to jump was ordered to keep the parachute on his back after landing. The unfortunate man then had to walk through the camp, advertising his change of heart. These last minute nerves could be fatal. Men who failed at the first attempt were given a second chance and sometimes a third. DuVivier remembers one recruit who was on his last chance. 'But he couldn't do it, so I told him to unhook [the static line] and go and sit at the front. That was him finished. But when he saw his mates all going out he suddenly changed his mind and jumped. Unfortunately, he rushed out without hooking himself up.'

They also had specialist engineers, under the command of Captain Bill Cumper, to instruct on explosives. They familiarized themselves with primers, detonators, igniters, explosive cords, safety fuses and booby trap appliances. They learned how to calculate the amount of explosive needed for different jobs, how to use pressure switches and the difference between a blasting charge and a cutting charge. Then there were the navigational skills to contend with. Each man had to be capable of finding his way to a target or back to his base, on his own initiative. The most gruelling part of their training was the route marches. These were normally 30 miles long and taught the men how best to conserve both energy and that most precious of commodities, water. They learned not to drink before midday, to rinse their mouths with small sips, never to gulp and never lend your water to your friend, which was considered a sure way to make enemies and destroy morale.

No such restrictions applied when the men were off-duty, of course – then you could gulp all the drink you could afford. A night in the Navy mess was usually filled with good-humoured banter and high jinks, and their hosts were a tolerant lot. As well as the Navy mess, there were evening trips to Suez to be had in one of the 3-ton trucks that raced each other at breakneck speeds, up and down the canal road. Suez was less exciting then the capital, but a pleasant evening could be spent nevertheless, in the small cafes and bars dotted around the port. Egyptian beer and spirits were cheap and of course there was the locally brewed hard-tack, 'Blue Nile', which, according to one of the last surviving veterans, Bob Lawson, 'only the Irish would drink.'

Alternatively, a few hours entertainment could be had at a nearby picture house run by the enterprising 'Shafto'. This was a large timber structure through which the sand and wind billowed freely. The reels frequently broke down and the ice cream and beer on offer was somewhat suspect. Occasionally, the men were given short leave passes to Cairo. These nights out would often end up involving the Military Police, and a night in their cells often ensued. However, unless the charges were extremely serious, the offenders were sent back to camp the next day. The Regiment's reputation had spread by now, and the men were usually cut some slack. On one such occasion Paddy Mayne had already knocked out a provost marshal and six Redcaps, before he was eventually arrested at Shepheard's Hotel. He was bundled away to the cells only to be released next morning by order of MEHQ, much to the annoyance of the embarrassed provost marshal. This was only one of a long series of skirmishes between the fiery second-in-command and the Redcaps.

Shafto's snacks were not the only health hazard for the soldiers. Desert sores were a constant problem, sometimes necessitating a spell in hospital. They started out usually as a cut or scratch that became infected by insect bites. The infection soon worsened and it became extremely difficult to get rid of. The sores often showed on the face and hands, where the skin was more exposed to the elements. At least the Regiment now had its own medical facility and if dressing and cleaning the sores brought no improvement, the patient was hospitalized for a few weeks. Another annoying aspect of camp life was the constant problem of bed bugs. They thrived in the desert heat and seemed resistant to all methods of extermination. The men kept clean with morning showers, but in the evening most preferred to swim in the Bitter Lake (by then the shower water was usually scalding, having had the desert sun on the tanks all day). Sports tournaments were organized in basketball, rugby, football and of course boxing. There were regular issues of cigarettes (in round tins of fifty 'Players') and rum. An added bonus of life in Kabrit was the use of many German and Italian prisoners as servants – though the Germans were unenthusiastic about the arrangement.

Stirling was now growing impatient to have another crack at Benghazi and set up a new base camp at Siwa oasis with this in mind. In ancient times, Siwa city was renowned for its splendour, and in its heyday it had played host to Alexander the Great and Cleopatra. It was now run-down and crumbling with neglect. It lay at the northern tip of the Great Sand Sea, halfway between Kabrit and Benghazi and already provided a base for the LRDG. On 21 May Stirling set out in the Blitz Buggy, with regular sidekicks Johnny Cooper and Reg Seekings. They had both arrived in Cairo with the 7 Commando and were among the first batch of men selected for L Detachment. He also brought along, for reasons best known to himself, Randolph Churchill. Also on board was Conservative MP, Fitzroy MacLean, who had joined up along with Churchill and two of his men, Rose and Alston. With them, they had an LRDG patrol to help navigate the journey. Leaving the LRDG at the designated rendezvous, they ran into a roadblock outside the town. Luckily, the Italian guards fell for the Blitz Buggy's German markings and MacLean's limited Italian, with which he admonished them for their sloppy appearance. The guards promptly saluted their 'superiors' and they drove on towards the harbour. Their plan was to sink whatever they found of importance there, but it turned out that the inflatables they had brought for the purpose had been punctured during the rough desert crossing, so the mission was aborted. Having made it safely back to Siwa, Stirling then crashed the Blitz Buggy en route to Cairo. Although he himself escaped with a broken wrist, the *Daily Telegraph* war correspondent Arthur Merton, who had hitched a lift with them, was killed, MacLean suffered a fractured skull, and Randoph Churchill was invalided out with a back injury – a rather inglorious end to any hopes his father might have had that he would make a name for himself, as Winston himself had done in a previous war.

Back in Cairo, Stirling heard the latest news and it wasn't good. Rommel was gaining the upper hand in the desert fighting and the Allies were in retreat. Meanwhile, Malta was close to capitulation. Enemy submarines and dive-bombers were constantly sinking the convoys sent to relieve the island. If Malta fell, the Germans would have free reign over the Mediterranean. Auchinleck now made plans for an offensive to coincide with the departure of two relief convoys on 13 June. At the same time, several units of L Detachment would raid Benghazi and the surrounding airfields, where many of the aircraft used to attack the convoys were kept. Stirling's group would raid Benina aerodrome, Mayne, with his men, would attack Berka Satellite, and a unit of fifteen Free French were allocated Derna and Martuba. This unit was under the command of Lieutenant Augustin Jordan, and as well as his compatriots it also contained a group of German Jews and two captured Germans. They had apparently seen the error of their ways, changed sides and been cleared by British Intelligence. They would wear captured Afrika Korps uniforms and arrive at their target in German trucks. At the same time Lieutenant George Jellicoe, the Conservative MP and future minister, would lead a daring raid on Heraklion aerodrome in Crete, from where the dive-bombers also operated. The Axis could still mount attacks from their Italian bases, which were nearer to Malta, and the SAS were powerless to prevent them. However, as Stirling impressed upon the men, if they managed to put a bomb on even just one plane the whole fleet would have to be grounded as a precaution.

Again they used Siwa oasis as a starting point. This time, Stirling took only Reg Seekings and Johnny Cooper, both recently promoted to the rank of sergeant. As the Blitz Buggy neared their target Stirling told Seekings; 'If I go down, you and John carry on. Don't worry about me, just go. If John goes down, you go. Get that bomb on, get one, that's all we ask ... Malta's more important than we are.' He needn't have worried. Sneaking beyond the perimeter in total darkness they managed to destroy both aircraft and hangars. As they made good their escape, they halted at a guardhouse. They listened briefly to the carefree banter inside, before Stirling calmly opened the door and rolled a grenade along the floor. As they pulled away the place exploded.

Jordan's party, meanwhile, had reached their target in previously captured German trucks and managed to clear several checkpoints undetected. Having hidden out until nightfall they split into two groups, one going on to Martuba while Jordan's truck headed for Derna. As they pulled up at a hangar, one of the Germans riding in front got out and headed towards the door. The men in the back thought little of this until they heard a commotion outside. Realizing they had been betrayed, they opened fire and hoped for the best. The end result was that only Jordan made it back to the rendezvous, on foot. The lorry, loaded with ammunition, had blown up during the firefight and all his men had either been killed or captured. The man who sealed their fate, referred to in *Stirling's Men* as 'Herr Bruckner' and thought to have been formerly with the French Foreign Legion, was soon on his way to Berlin where he was awarded the Deutsche Kreuz Gold – two grades higher than the Iron Cross.

Paddy Mayne took three tried and trusted men to Berka. With Jimmy Storie, Bob Lilley and Arthur Warburton he managed to see off fifteen planes before things got too hot. Warburton was eventually captured after several days, but the others got out safely. Stirling, Mayne and a few others then had the gall to drive back to Benina to admire their handiwork. On their way back they couldn't resist the temptation of a bunch of German and Italian soldiers drinking outside a roadhouse. They drew up alongside and emptied their machine guns into the crowd. When George Jellicoe arrived back in Kabrit several days later he had with him only one of the Greek Sacred Squadron. Arriving by submarine with just five men, they had succeeded in destroying twenty-one dive-bombers. However, three men were captured and one killed. Jellicoe, who had only joined up in April was later awarded the DSO for his efforts. Back at Siwa, L Detachment reviewed their latest work. They had destroyed some seventy planes in total, as well as inflicting dozens of casualties. Relaxing in the sweet-water springs and surrounded by date palms, Stirling was pleased. He felt sure they had done enough to save Malta and, as he learned later, they had. The convoys had been heavily attacked, as predicted, causing one to turn back. However, the remaining convoy sailed on to Malta and, though only two ships made it to port, the supplies they carried were enough to save the day. Stirling was adamant, with some justification, that an extra seventy aircraft would have sunk the lot. What he heard over the radio that evening however, shook him out of any complacent thoughts he may have been entertaining. The date was 21 June 1942 and the war in the desert was not going well. Tobruk had finally surrendered and Cairo itself was preparing for the worst. In a period that became known as 'the Flap', the order was given to burn all Army records and most of the affluent residents had already deserted their city. The RAF ordered their bombing squadron to relocate to Palestine. The Navy began to evacuate from Alexandria, and Suez was chock-a-block with warships waiting for orders to sail. The Germans were already minting medals to celebrate the end of the African campaign and Mussolini and his white charger were patiently waiting at Derna to lead the victory parade through Cairo. L Detachment and the LRDG both evacuated their Siwa base without delay, Stirling heading for Cairo once more while the rest returned to Kabrit. One week later the Axis thrust came to a halt at a small railway siding called El Alamein – a name that was soon to go down in history.

Chapter Six

'Up the Blue' with L Detachment

Of the L Detachment men on their first job, Chris O'Dowd stood out. 'He was a bloody good soldier,' (Bill) Seekings remembered. The 22-year-old Irishman was a joyful and untamed spirit. A night out in Cairo with O'Dowd was always uproarious.

Gavin Mortimer, Stirling's Men

The capture of Tobruk pleased Hitler so much that he immediately promoted Rommel to the rank of field marshal. On the Allied side, Auchinleck dismissed General Ritchie and took command of the Eighth Army himself. Meanwhile, Stirling used his time in Cairo to excellent effect. He had got wind of a recent delivery of American 'Willie Bantam' jeeps, and within a few days had managed to appropriate fifteen, plus a fleet of 3-ton Ford trucks. While there was speculation in some quarters that this was payback by Churchill for putting up with his son, there is a more feasible explanation for all the doors that were suddenly being opened for Stirling. At around this time he had enjoyed dinner and a chinwag with Churchill, Auchinleck, and all the top generals at the British Embassy. Never a man to miss an opportunity, the SAS commander passed around a folded page of paper and asked the elevated company to autograph it, in honour of the momentous occasion. The men obliged and were politely thanked. Later Stirling filled in the top of the paper to make it look like an official letter, granting permission to his Regiment to have whatever supplies and equipment they desired.

Though Stirling was not to know it at the time, this latest windfall would prove to be the making of the SAS. What he did realize, however, was that he was at last in a position to achieve one of his original key principles for the Regiment, namely independence. While he was perfectly happy to work with the LRDG, it was obvious that both groups would operate more efficiently by being independent of each other. Still on the lookout for more equipment, Stirling then got hold of a dozen of the fastest firing guns in the Middle East. The Vickers K machine guns came from scrapped Gloster Gladiator biplanes and had a firing rate of 1,200 rounds per minute. He also acquired some high-calibre Brownings, for good measure. He then managed to enlist the cooperation of a Royal Electrical and Mechanical Engineers (REME) workshop near Heliopolis, for the purpose of mounting them on the jeeps. Reg Seekings was sent to oversee the job and he got on famously with the big Irishman in command – this despite having tossed him out of a jeep during a test drive, after which the Irishman declared Seekings to be 'mad as a hatter'. Over the space of a couple of weeks they worked into the small hours fitting the jeeps out with the guns. Armour plates were added to protect the radiators and windscreens from scrapped Hurricanes to give better cover. Condensers were added and extra racks for equipment. Then the springs had to be reinforced because of the extra weight. Finally the jeeps had to be camouflaged. Seekings was not satisfied with the results, believing the colours to be too dull for the desert. When he brought this to the attention of the boss he was told, 'Here's the tools, do it yourself.' Seekings had picked up on the LRDG's use of pastel colours for desert transport, but when the mechanics saw the pink, blue, green and yellow jeep he finally produced, they fell about laughing. The SAS man had the last laugh, however, when the jeep was put against the desert backdrop and viewed from a distance. To Seekings' delight, it became almost invisible.

On first impressions the Willys had appeared lightweight compared to the Chevrolet trucks operated by the LRDG. Although they had four-wheel drive, they could only take two men and looked small in comparison. By the time the first batch was delivered to Kabrit however, they had been transformed. Now mounted with a twin Vickers K, front and back, plus a Browning machine gun for the driver, the jeeps were a formidable sight. The men were immediately put on a crash-course, and took to their latest task with unbridled enthusiasm. This was a real shot in the arm for men who had waved goodbye to their Navy's ships, as they withdrew from the Suez a few weeks earlier. The new men, in particular, were feeling cheated. Having worked so hard to gain their wings, it was looking like a full-scale retreat might be their first action with the Regiment. Among the new men, Chris was more than eager to have a crack at this new-fangled truck and, by extension, at the Germans. Over the following days men and jeeps were put through their paces, racing up and down embankments, learning the intricacies of the steering and trying out the guns. Any doubts they may have had about the Vickers K were quickly dispelled when they were fired. The racket they made was sufficient to put the wind up the most hardened of sentries. The jeeps were quicker than they looked and relatively easy to manoeuvre. The men were now itching to go.

They need not have fretted. Stirling soon arrived back in Kabrit and was suitably impressed by what he saw. Within days he called his band of brothers together and announced his latest plans. He would need fifty men, he told them, to operate from a remote spot in the desert. From there, they would raid several airfields at the same time and also attack the supply lines. They were to stay at their base camp for as long as it took to inflict maximum damage. Any new man who had gained his wings and was fit would be welcome to tag along. There was no shortage of volunteers and amongst the names on the final list was Chris's. At last he would have a chance to prove he was the right man for the job he had always wanted. Stirling then took time to talk to his men, especially those on their first job. He listened to what they had to say and offered encouragement in return. After a visit to the sergeants' mess he sped off once more, this time for Alexandria. He was due for a meeting at HQ on the next day and it was from there that the Regiment would set out, after first collecting their commander. Having already heard that Rommel's assault appeared to be floundering, what he would hear at HQ would be even more encouraging. The Desert Fox had stretched his supply lines to the limit in his effort to push the Allies further east and capture Egypt. His troops were only 60 miles from Alexandria, but it was a case of 'so near, yet so far' for the Afrika Korps. The Auk had chosen his defensive line carefully. The Eighth Army was holding firm at El Alamein, which was basically a 30-mile bottleneck. It was naturally defended to the north by the sea, and to the south by the inhospitable Qattara Depression. Auchinleck now planned an offensive for 7 July, to retake the coastal area around Mersa Matruh, and the SAS were to start the ball rolling by raiding the enemy airfields in the immediate vicinity. While the men were getting ready at Kabrit, Stirling and Auchinleck were finalizing plans at HQ.

Kabrit became a hive of activity before Stirling had even left. The rest of the day flew by as men lined up outside the quartermaster's tent to draw their kit. They eventually emerged laden down with emergency rations, water bottles and compasses. Others were picking out their choice of weapon from the vast array of automatics and revolvers at the armourer's store. Having decided, they then descended on the firing range to try them out. Back at the garage, the mechanics and fitters were putting the vehicles through their paces and making last minute adjustments. When the packs and blankets were loaded up, the men retired to the mess for what would be their last beer for some time. Each of the fifty-odd men picked for the job knew full well the implications of what they were about to embark on – it would have been made crystal clear to every man during basic training: any man unlucky enough to become a burden on his troop through injury would be left where he lay, to take his chances with nothing more than a bottle of water and his weapon. Reg Seekings remembered such occasions: 'I hated doing it, absolutely hated it, but it was my job. If you're doing a hard job and a tough job, you've got to be hard and tough yourself. You've got to make yourself callous, otherwise you're not going to survive, you'll go round the bend.' 'Gentleman' Jim Almonds had been a policeman in peacetime Britain before eventually ending up with the 8 Commando. While he described such occasions as being 'brutal', he realized their necessity: 'It's quite obvious you cannot travel with somebody who's seriously wounded, over probably a thousand miles of desert, bumping about in a truck. It's not possible.'

The next morning, 3 July, L Detachment set out in six 3-ton trucks and a dozen jeeps, bound for Cairo. Despite not knowing where they were going to finally end up, or how long their mission would last, the men were in high spirits as they reached the city. While the locals were used to the comings and goings of Allied convoys, this latest band of mavericks drew much attention as they edged their way through the city's traffic, armed to the teeth and singing at the top of their voices. While their bush jackets, shorts and desert boots

70

were army issue, they looked different to the normal tommy. None of the men wore the usual tin hat, while many were garbed in their preferred Arab headdresses. Having negotiated their way through the thronged and narrow streets, they proceeded to the outskirts of Alexandria and set up camp for the night. Arriving at HQ the next day, they met up with Stirling and Captain Robert (known as Robin) Gurdon of the LRDG. He would guide them to a remote spot on the northwestern edges of the Qattara Depression, a place considered to be impassable, where the LRDG already had a base. Turning south into the open desert, the heavily loaded lorries were soon getting bogged down in the shifting sands. By the time they set up camp for the night it had already been decided that two lorries would have to return to Kabrit the next day. They would take back as much extra provisions as the remaining party felt they could do without. It was a disappointing end to the adventure for those detailed to return with the trucks, but it had to be done.

When they woke the next morning the men were soaked through. A low-lying mist had descended and was causing havoc for the drivers as they tried to coax their engines to life. Having seen off their returning comrades, the main party then continued deeper into the desert. Chris and his buddies were now well and truly 'up the blue', as the more experienced men liked to call their time in the desolate terrain. They had set out wearing greatcoats and blankets as they drove through freezing fog. By midday, however, the fog had lifted and it became extremely hot. It was at this point they passed through the Eighth Army positions, waving and shouting at each other as they sped by.

Continuing in a westerly direction they made camp that night, choosing the driest ground available. The next morning they made good progress and soon reached the edge of the Qattara Depression. It was a totally barren landscape, where the only sign of human existence was a dirt track euphemistically called the Palm Leaf Road, which wound its way along the rim. Every now and then they came across the carcass of a long-dead camel. Looking down to the south, the cliffs fell away to reveal vast plains a thousand feet below them. After a tortuous day's driving they finally reached the LRDG base at Qaret Tartura. They had covered nearly 400 miles since leaving Kabrit. Having hidden the transport among the hills, they cooked their rations and ate around the campfire. Stirling announced that the action would begin next day so the men, already exhausted, were soon unrolling their blankets, and all had an early night for once.

Detailing the plans next morning, Stirling was his usual calm self. There were to be three separate raiding parties and all three attacks were scheduled to begin at midnight. George Jellicoe would lead a small party of a few jeeps northeast towards El Daba. Their orders were to strafe any convoys that happened to use the road and also to keep an eye out for Rommel, who was thought to be in the area. Another small combined patrol of SAS and LRDG would travel in a northwesterly direction to Sidi Barrani. The airstrip there was only used for refuelling and it was likely to be inactive. If this were the case, they would hide out, stay in radio contact and report on any enemy movements.

The largest group would attack Bagoush and Fuka airfields. This consisted of Stirling and Mayne, whose group would go on to raid Bagoush after leaving the main group at Fuka. There were three units in the main group: a unit of French under Lieutenant Augustin Jordan; another led by Arthur Sharpe, an ex-RAF officer; and a third under the command of Bill Fraser. Chris was chosen as part of the latter. The rendezvous would be at a place called Bir Chalder, which was 30 miles to the north. The next few hours were spent cleaning weapons, checking the engines and rationing out the petrol, food and water. Jellicoe's group then hit the road and the other groups soon followed suit, each taking their own direction. For Chris's unit this entailed travelling northwards along the track to Qara Matruh until they came to Bir Chalder. Here they turned off in a north-easterly direction and headed for Fuka. Soon they were coming across the burnt-out derelict wrecks of Allied lorries, abandoned in retreat. Suddenly there was a shout of 'Jerries!' from the driver in front. They stopped immediately and watched as a large convoy crossed their path about a mile away. As they faded into the desert, Stirling took the opportunity to issue some last minute advice. 'From now on you must keep your eyes skinned for enemy aircraft and armoured cars,' he told his men. 'Remember that we are targets for British as well as enemy planes, and if we are attacked and separated you must all drive on towards the airfields. Remember that! Nobody turns back. If we have to take evasive action, we must still head northwards for our objectives. It will be all right,' he reassured them, 'but keep wide awake. Now let's get going!'

On they went until they saw a cluster of tents away in the distance. On closer inspection they realized it was an outpost of the enemy lines. Making a detour, they kept the encampment carefully in their sights to make certain they had not been discovered. At sundown they reached the edge of a huge escarpment from where they could see Fuka airfield below them in the distance. At this point Stirling and Mayne wished the main party good luck and set off towards their own target at Bagoush. It was the first time the two men would be together on a raid. With them as usual was Johnny Cooper.

After skirting around a minefield, the main unit managed to motor down the escarpment, making a terrible racket in the process. The noise created by the revving engines and skidding wheels was enough to alert any nearby enemy. However, they managed to reach the bottom undetected. Driving on, they finally stopped a couple of miles from the lights of the airfield. Between them and the target was the railway line from Alexandria to Matruh, while beyond the airfield lay the main coastal road. They congratulated the navigators on being ahead of schedule and sat around the trucks eating cold sausage, all the time watching and listening. Shortly before midnight the men began to sling the bombs on their belts and check their weapons. After some final words of advice, Bill Fraser led his men into the darkness and towards the lights of Fuka. The remaining groups took off at five-minute intervals, Sharpe's patrol heading for a satellite airstrip nearby. Four men remained behind to guard the transport and guide the units back to base.

Fraser's unit reached the sentry posts unchallenged. The plan now was to sneak past the guards and make their way to the planes without giving the game away. This was the usual *modus operandi*; the French however had different ideas. They decided to stroll up to the gates and pass themselves off as being German. Having been challenged and discovered, they scarpered into the darkness while pandemonium broke out all around the airfield. Chris and his mates were crawling in the dirt between two sentry posts when the rattle of the Breda gun and the shouts of the Italian guards shattered the quiet night. Realizing that the game was well and truly up, Fraser gave the whispered order for his men to retrace their steps and abort the mission. There was no point in trying to fight their way on to the airfield. They would have been outgunned, and eventually killed or captured. They managed to get away, and were soon heading towards the torch beam that flickered at thirty-second intervals, to guide them back to the transport. As they got their breath back the other two patrols arrived. The French had managed to blow up nine planes despite giving the game away, while the raid on the satellite airfield had grounded another six. This did little to console Fraser, however, who was livid with the French for not following orders. Their reprimand would have to wait, however. It was now approaching 1500 hrs and time to get as far away as possible before dawn. This was the stage of a raid that all the men dreaded, including Reg Seekings: 'If you'd a clear run, going in was easy. Coming out was the problem. You had to clear an area. You could hide from a bomber; they were slower, you could fight them off. But you couldn't with fighters. Once they pointed their nose at you, it was rough.'

After managing to scale the escarpment they were faced with a difficult decision: they could waste a lot of time edging along the narrow path that surrounded the minefield, or they could take a chance and drive through it. They decided on the latter course of action and fortunately the mines were not fused. They were making good progress, when one of the lorries broke down. As the men stood around the stricken vehicle there was a sudden cry of 'aircraft!' There was just enough time to take cover before the two German fighters came skimming across the sands at a height of no more than 50 feet. The men froze where they were, most using the transport as cover. They waited as the noise dissipated, fearing its return. Their luck held however: The enemy pilots had most likely presumed that their little convoy of two lorries and a jeep were derelict, part of the wreckage left behind by the retreating Allies. It was high time to hide out for the day, as this latest incident had proved. A sense of urgency now prevailed and the truck was quickly repaired. They then went on for a few miles until they found enough desert scrub to afford some protection. The jeep was hidden among the bushes and covered with camouflage, but the trucks were too large. Instead the men left them in the open at peculiar angles with the bonnets raised. Hoping this would make them look like wrecks from the air, the men lay down and fell asleep.

At noon they decided to move on, praying the haze brought on by the midday sun would be sufficient to disguise the convoy. Heading in a southwesterly direction, they reached the rendezvous at Bir Chalder that evening. Stirling, Mayne, and Cooper were already

74

there, and rejoiced in their comrades' safe return. But soon afterwards the peace was shattered yet again by the familiar shout of 'aircraft!' This time they had been spotted, even as they ran for cover. A machine-gun battle immediately ensued and lasted until the lone CR 42 had run out of ammunition, at which point, unable to inflict any more damage, it headed north over the skyline. Stirling for once lost his cool when he discovered the Blitz Buggy had been strafed, but otherwise there was little damage and no casualties. However, their position would be reported and they would have to think about a new hideout very soon. Jellicoe's unit returned shortly before sunset, closely followed by the SAS/LRDG group, who had been under Robin Gurdon's command. They reported at least twenty trucks destroyed and while Jellicoe's troop had been less successful they had taken three German prisoners. It was then time to assess the success of the mission. While it was impossible to be sure of the exact numbers, each patrol gave their best estimation. The Fuka patrol claimed fifteen planes destroyed, while Stirling put the number accounted for at Bagoush as about thirty. However, Stirling's strategy was to always be conservative with the tally, when reporting to HQ. In that way, his remaining enemies at Cairo could never accuse him of exaggerating. He therefore scaled down the total to thirty planes. By morning the RAF would send a reconnaissance plane to view the damage, another good reason to err on the side of caution. As they toasted their latest success with a flagon of army issue rum, Stirling advised an early night. The enemy would most likely come hunting for them at first light. They would have to leave their hideout before then.

At 0300 hrs the guards woke up their comrades and the convoy was soon speeding on a northeasterly bearing. They crossed the Matruh Qara track and made good progress from there. With daylight beckoning, they found their spot in the shape of a small escarpment known as Bir al-Quseir. They drove the trucks and jeeps down the steep slopes and hid them among wadis and rocks at the bottom. Camouflage nets and scrub were used to finish the process. Only then could the men enjoy breakfast and a little peace of mind. A few days later Jellicoe and Gurdon led another attack on El Daba, hoping for a better result this time. It was not to be, however. The convoy was strafed and bombed en route, and lost all its vehicles but one. Robin Gurdon was killed and was buried where he fell. The nine remaining men eventually made it back to base in one jeep.

On 11 July a large patrol, which included Chris, returned to Fuka and accounted for another twenty aircraft. In between these raids, the men had few duties beyond any running repairs the transport needed, and keeping their guns clean and oiled. There was always time for a chat and a game of cards in some shady spot out of the sun. By noon the desert was scorching hot, but at night and in the early morning it was often very cold. To cope with these extremes, the men wore little more than shorts by day, while at night they wrapped themselves in greatcoats and blankets to fend off the bitter cold.

By now all were bearded and some had unsightly desert sores. They bore little resemblance to the conventional tommy, but barrack room discipline was no longer their concern. They shared the landscape with gazelles, jackals, foxes and jerboas – all capable survivors in this terrain, despite the absence of an obvious water supply. Snakes, scorpions and chameleons scurried around in the nearby scrub and sometimes became unwelcome guests in the camp. After the evening meal of bully beef the men were given their next day's water ration, which they buried in the sand for optimum coolness. Next came the issue of rum and lime, which was always in plentiful supply. These were the hours most eagerly anticipated by the men. As the moon rose they gathered around and filled their mess tins from the flagon jars of rum. After some banter, the night usually ended up in a singsong. Malcolm Pleydell, who was also on his first 'job' as patrol medic, wrote glowingly of these musical soirees. He recalls how even the German prisoners were persuaded to join in on one occasion. Most preferred songs of the sentimental variety such as 'My Melancholy Baby' or 'I'll never Smile Again'. Another favourite was the English version of 'Lili Marlene'. The song had come to Egypt with the Afrika Korps, but the Tommies had it translated and it soon became popular among the troops. Colonel Mayne liked it so much that he penned his own version and it eventually became the official Regimental song. But the session was never complete without some Scottish and Irish songs being thrown into the mix. Here Pleydell describes the beginnings of such an event:

Paddy Mayne stretched out beside me and speaking little; David Stirling, George Jellicoe and a few others grouped together further down the slope; the French in an animated chattering circle; and the Germans nearby ... A memory of the atmosphere of men; the deep jumble of voices; the sound of a laugh that seemed to hang in the air for a fraction of a second before it was lost in the night; the yellow flame of a match lighting up a man's bearded face, throwing the features into sharp relief, sketching in the lines with deep shadows; the brighter glow of ruby red as he drew on his cigarette. The men themselves; some hunched forward, talking eagerly; some joking; some lying back quietly ... Soon a fresh song would start up and everything else would be lost in it. You would hear the individual voices of those near to you; you would smile to yourself as they tried to reach the higher notes. But beyond them it was just a wall of sound. And beyond that again it was the blank emptiness of the desert, milky and pale as it stretched away faintly into the silent gloom. We had formed a small solitary island of voices; voices which faded and were caught up in the wilderness. A little cluster of men singing in the desert. An expression of feeling that defied the vastness of its surroundings. For we might have been in the mess, we might have been in a pub at home, we might have been in a crowd waiting for a football match to start.

While he enjoyed these evenings as much as the next man, Stirling's mind was always focused on what lay ahead, and the raid on Bagush had most certainly given him food for thought. As a result of what happened that night, the SAS were to change their tactics and become an even greater menace to the Führer. When they had reached Bagoush, Mayne and a small group headed for the airfield, while Stirling and two men set up a roadblock. Mayne was making good progress and had already accounted for about fifteen planes, when he realized that some of the Lewes bombs were not exploding. On closer inspection it was evident that the primers had become damp and he decided to abort the raid. After returning to Stirling's group however, the two men made an instant decision. The twin Vickers had, after all, been designed as an anti-aircraft weapon. They drove straight back to the airfield, counting on the presumption that the enemy would not be expecting so audacious a move. The gamble worked perfectly. As the Blitz Buggy and jeep cruised along between the lines of aircraft, the gunners aimed for their fuel tanks. It took no more than five minutes to destroy thirty-seven planes. They escaped with no more damage than a few singed eyebrows from the inferno they had caused, and there seemed no reason why the same tactics would not work again.

SAS song of the Regiment
(Lyrics by Colonel Blair 'Paddy' Mayne)

There was a song we always used to hear,
Out in the desert, romantic, soft and clear
Over the ether, came the strain,
That soft refrain, each night again,
To you Lili Marlene, to you Lili Marlene.

(Chorus)
Then back to Cairo we would steer,
And drink our beer, and ne'er a tear,
And poor Marlene's boyfriend
Will never see Marlene.

Check you're in position, see your guns are right,
Wait until the convoy comes creeping through the night,
Now you can pull the trigger, son,
And blow the Hun to Kingdom come,
And Lili Marlene's boyfriend will never see Marlene.

Twenty thousand rounds of tracer and of ball,
Forty thousand rounds of the stuff that makes 'em fall,
Finish your strafing, drive away,
And live to fight another day,
But Lili Marlene's boyfriend will never see Marlene.

Creeping into Fuka, forty planes ahead,
Belching ammunition, and filling them with lead,
A 'flamer' for you, a grave for Fritz,
He's like his planes, all shot to bits,
And Lili Marlene's boyfriend will never see Marlene.

Afrika Korps has sunk into the dust,
Gone are the Stukas, its Panzers lie in rust,
No more we'll hear that haunting strain,
That soft refrain, each night again,
For Lili Marlene's boyfriend will never see Marlene.

Chapter Seven

Return to Benghazi

'In a sense they weren't really controllable. They were harness-able. The object was to give them the same purpose. And that goal had to be an exacting one, because from the start we knew we would never make it as a regiment unless not only we operated effectively, but we succeeded in establishing a new role. And that band of vagabonds had to grasp what they had to do in order to get there.'

David Stirling on The Originals

By now supplies were running dangerously low and much of the transport needed replacing. While the jeeps had proved their worth, they had taken a battering in the harsh terrain and many were now rendered redundant. Stirling had no option but to return to Cairo to replenish his regiment. Having left some twenty men behind to guard their new hideout, Stirling and the rest set out across the Qattara Depression on their arduous journey home. They were unable to use the track to the north, as the Germans had destroyed it. Arriving more or less intact, he wasted no time in putting forward his new idea to HQ. His logic was sound: the SAS relied heavily on the element of surprise for their hit-and-run raids. Therefore, they could not allow any element of their attack, particularly their approach, to become too predictable. The enemy had changed their security methods as a result of the early raids, installing searchlights and barbed-wire fences. They had increased the guards and even deployed armoured cars at the main airstrips. It was time for a fresh approach as Stirling's New Tactics paper, which he now presented to HQ, made clear. He encountered little opposition from the usual nitpickers, on this occasion.

Meanwhile, his men were enjoying their well-earned rest back at Kabrit. Their evenings were spent either in the Navy mess or around the streets of Cairo. While there was always a good night guaranteed at the mess, the lure of the capital was ever-present during these periods of relaxation. For Christy, this was a time to savour. He had proven his worth on his first raid and given a good account of himself. Any doubts he may have had about his capabilities as an SAS man had been dispelled. According to Reg Seekings, you were never finally selected until you had been in action:

> That was the final test. It's an unknown quantity. You can train a man up, but you can't say how he'll react in the field. But a man that can undergo this hard mental and physical stuff and suffer without complaining, he's the most likely chap to survive. One chap there, he was one of the leading boxers in the world and would take on any amount of men with his hands. But the first bullet that went past his ear, he'd completely had it. It's the people who think about it who are most likely to succeed. It's a matter of conditioning yourself for it. If you're one of those who go in the pub and say, 'Give me a rifle and I'll go and shoot these buggers' – they're the sort of people who fold up.

Chris had certainly not folded in the heat of battle, nor was he likely to when challenged on a night out, it seems. Bob McDougall, who had joined up at the same time, remembered drinking with Chris in a bar when a loud-mouthed Aussie soldier took a dislike to the young Irishman and threw down a challenge to him. His account of the incident is given in Gavin Mortimer's book, *Stirling's Men*: 'They had a competition to see who could punch the hardest, the prize was a crate of Stella beer. The Aussie went first and hit O'Dowd so hard that his chin practically went round his head. O'Dowd just stood there. The Aussie looked at him, reached into his pocket for his wallet, paid for the crate, then buggered off.'

One week later they were all back at Bir al-Quseir, and seldom did a band of comrades receive a better welcome. Those who had stayed behind had been bored silly and were parched and half-starved by this stage. But now their mates had returned with ample supplies of water, food and rum as well as cigarettes, old magazines and even eau-de-cologne to make up for the absence of washing water.

Having celebrated their return that evening, the camp became a hive of activity at daybreak. Stirling had requisitioned another eighteen jeeps plus some 3-ton trucks, and cover had to be found nearby in which to hide them. While all this was in progress, Stirling had a radio message from HQ. It confirmed his suspicions that the airfield at Sidi Haneish was being used as an operating base for the dreaded Stuka dive-bombers. He decided to attack at the earliest opportunity. That night, the full complement of jeeps drove out into the desert for a dress rehearsal. They practised all night, forming into two columns with the jeeps driving ten yards apart. On a signal from Stirling, they opened fire with a devastating salvo of live ammunition. On through the night they tried out various formations, wheeling left and right as they fired on the imaginary targets. They made a deafening racket in the still night air, already hundreds of miles behind enemy lines. At first light Stirling finally seemed satisfied, and ordered his men to camouflage the transport and get some rest. They were to attack that night.

Although the target was only 40 miles away, they had some trouble with the navigation – this, despite the fact that they now had at their disposal an expert navigator named Mike Sadler, whom Stirling had poached from the LRDG. The convoy had halted to check their bearings when they were startled by the landing-lights of Sidi Haneish being suddenly turned on no more than a mile away. Stirling's first reaction was fear of betrayal, but he was soon reassured as a German plane made its approach to the runaway. The timing was perfect. The convoy was able to drive with lights out to within 200 yards of the perimeter and form into line abreast. Moments later Stirling shouted the order, 'Fire!' The din of forty-eight Vickers Ks firing 20,000 rounds per minute was earth-shattering. The first casualty was the Heinkel that had landed only moments earlier. Meanwhile, several men jumped from their jeeps to cut the perimeter fence. Stirling then pulled out in front while the rest formed into a double column, one led by Mayne, the other by Jellicoe. On the given signal they charged on to the field and drove along the rows of aircraft. The enemy troops cowered for cover, their only response being the constant rattle of a single Breda gun. The gunners let rip with both tracer and incendiary bullets, and the airfield soon resembled a scene from Dante's *Inferno*. The noise of the planes exploding was so deafening that it drowned out the guns. Reaching the end of line, the jeeps swung round and finished off what they had missed. Leaving the burning skeletons of the planes, they next turned their attention towards the bomb dumps and hangers. Then they withdrew, almost as quickly as they had arrived. The attack had lasted just fifteen minutes and they now had about three hours left before dawn. After driving some distance, the convoy stopped to take stock and to divide into separate groups. Their euphoria was immediately dampened upon learning that 21-year-old John Robson, a new recruit, had been shot through the head and lay dead in his jeep. After burying Robson, they broke into sections for the hazardous journey back to base.

As it turned out, Stirling's group were the last to make it back. They finally rolled up on the night of 28 July, a total of nine men hanging off a single clapped-out jeep. Stirling was immediately informed of the death of André Zirnheld of the Free French. He had been mortally wounded during a Stuka attack and had died on the journey back. Despite this loss of two men and several jeeps, the raid was an undoubted success. On a rough calculation they felt sure they had accounted for at least forty aircraft, but as usual Stirling brought down the official total to thirty. What was particularly pleasing to Stirling was the fact that along with the usual Stukas and Junkers, they had destroyed several JU 52s. These were used exclusively as supply planes and their loss would certainly slow Rommel down.

Buoyed up by this most recent success, Stirling was now prepared for a long and productive stay 'up the blue'. With this in mind, he requested another thirty jeeps from Cairo. He was astounded sometime later to receive orders for the entire force to return to Kabrit immediately. Most of the men were flown back on a Bombay that was originally meant to bring them supplies, while some remained behind to drive the transport. When Stirling arrived at HQ he quickly realized that he was at least partially to blame for the sudden order to withdraw. Following the last raid on Benghazi, he had submitted proposals for a fresh raid on the harbour. The idea was to scuttle a ship and to use it to block the entrance, thus trapping whatever shipping was already there while also preventing any new arrivals. He had discussed the plan with Colonel Haselden of the Intelligence Corps who had convinced his colleagues of its validity. However, in Stirling's absence the project had expanded into a large-scale assault involving soldiers from other units and even a couple of tanks.

At an Embassy Ball that evening he was to hear some more un-settling news, from no less a source than Winston Churchill him-self. The Prime Minister was reluctantly relieving Auchinleck from his duties and replacing him with General Harold Alexander. The Eighth Army also had a new commander-in-chief, General Bernard Montgomery. This 'double whammy' must have been something of a shock for the normally cool Stirling, though he couldn't let it show. The Auk had always looked after the SAS boss, while Montgomery was a stranger and had little reason to indulge him. Nevertheless, he could always count on Churchill's support, and impressed on him the need to establish the SAS as a permanent unit. Stirling was anxious that the top brass would not have the excuse to disband L Detachment when the North African campaign ended.

Auchinleck had managed to repel Rommel's forces at the first battle of El Alamein, and the Allies knew that the Desert Fox was now desperately short of supplies. The ports of Benghazi, Tobruk and Matruh, which were all in Axis control, were vital for his further advancement. Stirling's original plan, now to be known as 'Opera-tion Bigamy', would incorporate L Detachment, two LRDG patrols, a naval detachment and part of the Special Boat Section. Force X, as the whole group was called, would number over 200 men. A raid on Tobruk, led by Colonel Haselden, would be carried out simul-taneously. Despite the fact that he was to be in charge of the Benghazi raid, Stirling was not happy with the plan, feeling it was too cumbersome to be effective. Many of his men felt the same. It reminded them of the old Commando operations, which had left a bitter taste in the mouth. They would have to travel over 1,000 miles in a convoy of some eighty vehicles just to reach their target: the chances of arriving there unexpected were slim. Nevertheless, they had their orders and began preparing.

On 4 September the advance party, led by Paddy Mayne, set out on a 1,200-mile trip across some of the worst desert terrain in the world. Among the ranks of five officers and 118 men was Chris. For some unknown reason he had missed out on the Sidi Haneish raid, but he would play a crucial role at Benghazi. In twelve jeeps and six supply trucks they followed the Nile to Asyut, and from there they headed west to Kufra, on the southern edge of the Great Sand Sea, a distance of 850 miles. Here they rested for a few days among the lakes and palm trees, before heading northwards for another

650 miles towards Benghazi. It was only when they were en route that the men were briefed on their destination.

After a gruelling six days they stopped at a place called the Wadi Gamra, which was close enough to Benghazi, and set up camp. Here, they shared their surroundings with a group of Senussi shepherds and their flocks. The area was ideal for a hideout, providing plenty of scrub cover, and the Senussi could be trusted to keep quiet. The rest of the men turned up over the next two days; one section under Stirling and the other under Bill Cumper. Stirling's section had not had the best of luck. The two Honey tanks had given up just north of Kufra and Lieutenant Robert Ardley from the Royal Navy became the first casualty of the operation, when his jeep hit a mine. His SAS driver, Corporal James Webster, had sustained a serious leg injury and Malcolm Pleydell was left with no choice but to amputate, there and then in the middle of desert. The loss of Lieutenant Ardley was a serious blow to the operation, as he had been stationed at Benghazi harbour during the previous year and had an intimate knowledge of the place. There had been rumours in Cairo that the enemy were expecting an attack, which had worried Stirling. Before his arrival, Fitzroy MacLean had sent an Arab spy to check out Benghazi, and the report was not good. According to MacLean's man, the place was teeming with thousands of Italian and German troops and the perimeter had been mined. Stirling immediately radioed HQ with the disturbing news only to be told to 'ignore bazaar gossip and proceed as planned.'

Nonetheless, Stirling was reluctant to dismiss the information out of hand. If it was true, the SAS would be going in without its most valuable weapon – the element of surprise. He also decided to keep the news from the men, fearing it might damage morale. The initial plan was to attack Benghazi from several positions. However, at some point he changed his mind and decided to concentrate the assault at just one position, south of the town. Most accounts of the operation suggest his reasoning was based on his belief that they were expected.

On the morning of 13 September the usual preparations began. Stirling and his fellow officers had spent the previous evening poring over the maps and finalizing their plans. A small group of about a dozen men were detailed to seize a fort overlooking the escarpment outside the town. The fort had a wireless set and it was essential that it be destroyed before the guards could alert Benghazi.

Chris aged 10 (front row, third from left), at Gortjordan School. His pal, Mick Walsh, is sixth from left, second row

Chris shortly before leaving for London outside his home at Cahernabruck

City slickers. Chris (centre) with Martin on his right and an unknown friend, London, 1939

Chris in the uniform of the Irish Guards, 1940

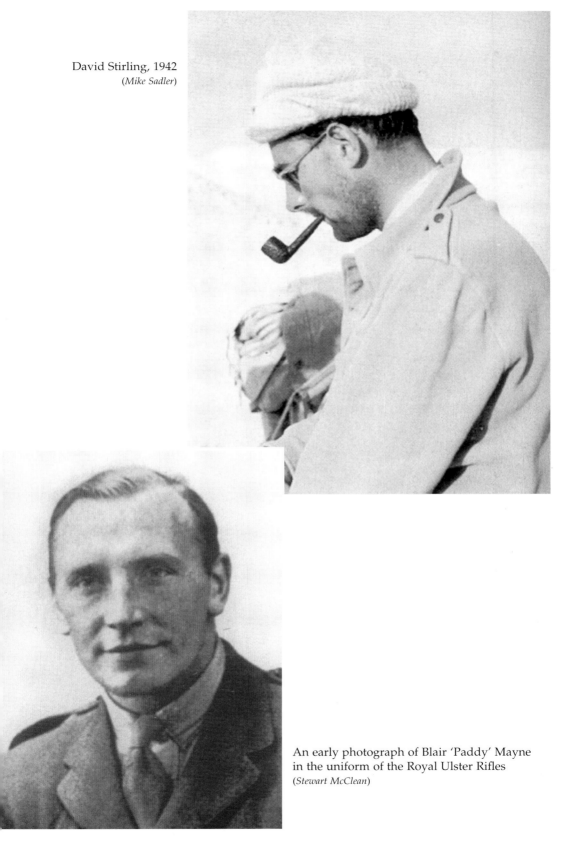

David Stirling, 1942
(*Mike Sadler*)

An early photograph of Blair 'Paddy' Mayne
in the uniform of the Royal Ulster Rifles
(*Stewart McClean*)

Blair Mayne during his university days (*S. McClean*)

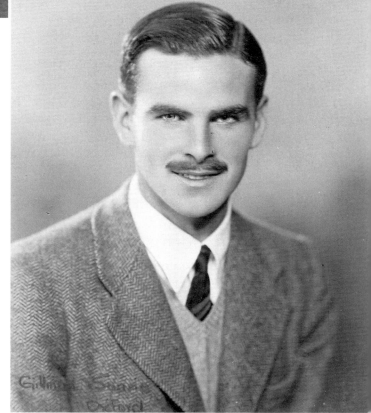

Jock Lewes, 1936
(*John Lewes*)

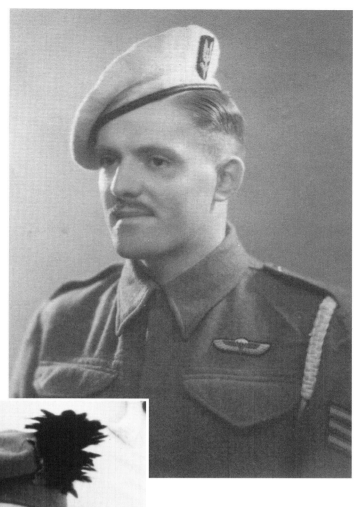

'Gentleman' Jim Almonds
in SAS uniform, 1941
(*Lorna Almonds-Windmill*)

'Paddy' Mayne wearing a
glengarry bonnet with a black
hackle, as worn by 11 Commando,
at Lamlash on the Isle of Arran
(*Duncan McAra*)

Colonel 'Paddy' Mayne in the desert
(*Mike Sadler*)

Bill Fraser, 1943
(*Gavin Mortimer*)

Going native – this picture (almost certainly) of Chris was recently discovered among some family papers. The outfit may have been used for undercover work, or was possibly just part of a tourist gimmick

On leave, Alexandria 1943 (*Deakin family estate*)

Bill Deakin (*Deakin family estate*)

Stirling making plans behind the lines with Jock Lewes (*John Lewes*)

L Detachment en route to a target (*Mike Sadler*)

Chris (left) with Johnny Rose and Jimmy Storie, Bir Zelten, 1942 (*Lorna Almonds-Windmill*)

Readying for a raid. Chris behind enemy lines at Bir Zelten in the Great Sand Sea, October 1942
(*G. Mortimer*)

Johnny Cooper (right) and Reg Seekings, enjoying a spot of leave in Cairo, 1941 (*Martin Dillon*)

Outside the ski school at Mount Hebron, early 1943. (Left to right) Vic Page, Chris O'Dowd, Chalky White, Johnny Rose and Tanky Thorne (*G. Mortimer*)

Johnny Wiseman (front row centre) and his troop pose for the camera in Sicily. Chris is third from the right, back row (*G. Mortimer*)

Special Raiding Squadron men relaxing after taking the defensive guns at Capo Murro di Porco (*S. McClean*)

The scene of devastation where Chris and eighteen of his comrades were killed in the battle for Termoli. The wreck of the truck they were boarding is on the left (*G. Mortimer*)

The site where Chris and his comrades were first buried in Termoli (*S. McClean*)

Chris's final resting place, Sangro River War Cemetery, Italy

Saluting the statue of Colonel Mayne at Newtownards, 2 May 1997. (Left to right) Jim Almonds, Jimmy Storie, Reg Seekings and Johnny Cooper (*Hamish Ross*)

Laying a wreath at the grave of Colonel Mayne at Newtownards, 2 May 1997. (Left to right) Johnny Cooper, Reg Seekings, Jim Almonds and Jimmy Storie (*Photo: H. Ross*)

Leading the group was a fifty-year-old Belgian, Bob Melot. Melot had worked in Alexandria between the wars and was a fluent Arabic speaker. He had also been a First World War fighter ace and was now proving his worth as a spy, mingling with the enemy while dressed as an Arab. His orders were to go in at 1600 hrs and to rejoin the main group within twenty minutes. He would then act as a guide for the main thrust of the attack. In charge of preparing the Lewes bombs was forty-year-old Captain Bill Cumper. A chirpy Cockney who had worked his way up the ranks, Cumper's usual occupation was training the recruits back at Kabrit and he was delighted to be on his first 'job'. While he distributed the bombs other men were busy stripping and cleaning the machine guns and readying the transport. As personal weapons the men carried Thompson sub-machine guns, .303 Lee-Enfields and an array of small arms. An escape kit consisting of a silk map, Benzedrine tablets and a button-compass was issued to each man.

Bob Melot's group left in the afternoon, followed by the main group just before sunset. The terrain was strewn with sharp rocks, which played havoc with the jeeps. En route, the medical crew branched off at a suitable spot and set up a base to treat the wounded, wishing good luck to their comrades. On reaching the fort, Melot attempted to bluff his way inside by speaking Italian. However, their cover was blown and a fierce gun battle ensued. Those who made it back to the main section reported that although the fort had been overrun, Melot and two others had been badly injured. This was bad news in every sense, given that the convoy was now without its designated guide and travelling in darkness. The RAF had arranged a diversionary bombing raid on the town for midnight, and they needed to be on time if they were to take full advantage. Inevitably, they lost their way and by the time they had descended the escarpment and approached Benghazi they were four hours behind schedule. The RAF had been and gone, and the approach road was barely discernible in the darkness. Stirling decided to switch on the jeep's lights and the convoy made its way cautiously onwards. The narrow road they found themselves on soon became bordered on either side by barbed wire, and the ground nearby looked suspiciously like a minefield. The first obstacle they came across was an unmanned roadblock. It consisted of no more than a single pole weighed down by a barrel. Bill Cumper and Stirling got out to have a look, Cumper keeping an eye out for mines. He verified that they were indeed surrounded by mines, although the roadblock itself wasn't booby-trapped. Satisfied that all was well, Cumper, ever the jester, lifted the pole, raised his arm in a mock-Nazi salute and announced, 'Let battle commence.'

Leading the attack was Jim Almonds' jeep. He was to take charge of the raid on the harbour and his vehicle was packed with explosives. With him up front was 'Maggie' McGinn. His rear gunner was a new man called Fletcher and he also had with him an Arab who knew the harbour. Almonds drove on until they came to a second roadblock, consisting of two concrete pillboxes with a cast iron chain stretched between them. As they came to a halt in front of it, all hell broke loose. A dozen or so machine guns opened up at point-blank range. Searchlights made them easy targets for a couple of Breda guns that were now rattling away on the other side. McGinn soon opened up with the twin Vickers, offering them a moment's respite, and at the first opportunity they dived off the jeep hoping to find some cover. Moments later the jeep and its cargo of limpets and Lewes bombs exploded in a huge fireball. Mortar shells were now raining down on the convoy, accompanied by sniper fire from some poplar trees nearby. Two jeeps, driven by Paddy Mayne and Jim Chambers, then screamed to a halt near the barrier and opened fire with everything they had. In Mayne's jeep, Chris was now in the thick of it, coaxing the twin Vickers K to its optimum performance. The firepower from the jeeps had the desired effect and provided a temporary buffer for the rest of the raiders. It also afforded Stirling enough time to gather his thoughts.

With daylight beckoning, he ordered the convoy to withdraw immediately. It would be futile to delay any longer, knowing that the enemy had plenty of reinforcements at the ready. Whatever chance they had of getting away would be gone as soon as dawn broke. Confusion now reigned as the men tried to turn the jeeps without straying on to the minefield. Any semblance of order was quickly lost amid the din of machine gun fire, explosions and revving engines. The wounded were quickly gathered up and loaded, as the convoy now entered a race against time. All the while the two jeeps stood firm, while Chris and the other gunners directed a devastating attack on their enemy. They went through drum after drum of ammunition, burning their fingers in the process of changing them. When the rest of the convoy had finally got a head start, Mayne gave the signal to withdraw. Chris and his fellow gunners gave one last long salvo as the drivers turned the jeeps and got them away. It was an orderless dash across open country to reach the shelter of the escarpment before first light. A game of cat and mouse ensued over the next twelve hours as the fragmented convoy dodged the enemy planes with varying degrees of success. They took shelter where they could, while above them the Stukas and Messerschmitts circled and swooped. Some flew alone, but often a group would contain up to twelve aircraft. They swooped at less than 200 feet and the men could clearly make out the insignia, whether German or Italian. Given a choice, they would have preferred to take their chances with the Luftwaffe. Whereas the Germans seemed satisfied with strafing and bombing the vehicles, the Italians tended to concentrate on the men themselves.

At midday there was an unexpected respite. After a cautionary look-round the men took advantage of the lull and emerged from their cover. Some had made it to the top of the escarpment by now, but most were some way up it or still waiting at the foot. Pleydell and his medical team busied themselves with the wounded, driving down the escarpment to tend to the different groups as they emerged from their makeshift shelters. Those who had succeeded in finding decent cover had avoided the worst ravages of the planes, but there were many casualties from the gun battle at Benghazi. Stirling and Seekings drove around all day collecting stragglers. Over the next few hours the bulk of the convoy made the 25-mile journey back to the Wadi Gamra, taking full advantage of the lull in air attacks. Malcolm Pleydell was relieved:

> Eventually we reached the rendezvous. It was about 3 o'clock in the morning. Wearily we got out of the lorries. The wounded were made comfortable. We dragged out our blankets and threw the camouflage nets loosely over the trucks. 'Home sweet home!' said a voice in the darkness. There was a half-hearted attempt at a laugh in response. 'Home sweet fucking home!' came the rejoinder. Silence in the wadi. A little breeze that tugged fitfully at the bushes. A deep sigh and a stretch of the legs. Then sleep, dear God, merciful sleep.

Pleydell and his team were away tending to more of the wounded the next day, when the wadi was attacked. They heard the explosions and gunfire, and saw the smoke rising from the wadi. A reconnaissance plane had spotted a single jeep driving towards the wadi, and the pilot soon returned with his friends. The jeep driver was ignoring orders by driving in daylight and there was a heavy price to pay for all concerned. Over the next few hours they were at the mercy of between twenty and thirty Axis planes as they came in wave after wave, saturating the wadi with bombs and bullets. To begin with the men returned fire and actually succeeded in bringing down an enemy plane. Such was the ferocity of the onslaught, however, that they eventually scattered out into the landscape, having first done their best to find shelter for the wounded who could not be moved. When the doctor and his team returned in the evening they viewed the devastation for themselves. The injured men had miraculously survived and casualties overall were light. The transport had borne the brunt of the attack, and all over the wadi were burning jeeps and trucks. Preparations were already being made to move out and this presented Stirling with a fresh problem. Having lost so many vehicles they now had barely enough room for the fit men, and making space for stretchers was out of the question. Furthermore, it was doubtful if the injured men would have the strength to last the 800-mile trip across such tough terrain.

Meanwhile the medical team drew lots to decide who would stay behind and take charge of the group. Melot's group had taken some prisoners at the entrance fort, one of whom happened to be a medical orderly. He was very relieved to hear that he was also to stay behind. Not so pleased were the injured themselves, many of whom were non-SAS and therefore not familiar with the Regiment's protocol on such occasions. Here Reg Seekings, who had brought back most of the casualties, including an old acquaintance from the regular Army, takes up the story:

> Well I was called back by I think it was a major, and he said: 'Sergeant, you've got men here that are dying if they don't get help.' And this friend of mine, he said: 'That's right, Reg. We'll die if we don't get help quick.' So I had to turn round and make the hardest little speech I'd ever made in my life. I said: 'I'm sorry, you've had it. You're just numbers. I've got twelve to fourteen men there. They're fit, they're ready to fight another day. If I can get 'em clear, they can carry on fighting. You can't, I'm sorry.' That was the hardest thing I ever had to do in my life. And I walked away and my pal started to call me 'Sergeant'

then, He was disgusted with me. I hated doing it, absolutely hated it, but it was my job.

In all, four of the injured were left behind. The remainder, including Bob Melot, were passed fit enough to take the long, rough ride back to Kufra. As the convoy prepared to leave, Pleydell issued some final instructions to his orderly. They were to make their way to Benghazi under the Red Cross flag, in order to get the men hospitalized. An unarmed jeep had been left behind for the purpose, along with adequate medical supplies. The main group then divided in two, as it was felt they would make better progress and be less obvious from the air. As night drew in, the first group headed out under the command of Paddy Mayne. The second group, commanded by Major Barlow, followed soon after. Stirling was not in either group. He had decided to remain in the area, but away from the wadi, in order to pick up any remaining stragglers. There were still some twenty men unaccounted for, so he took with him three jeeps and a half-dozen men. He also brought a wireless set to keep in touch with command. By now the rations were sparse, making the return trip a more daunting prospect for all concerned. Food intake was restricted to one evening meal and each man had one water bottle per day.

Arriving back at Kufra some six days later, Chris would have had his fill of desert fighting for a little while. He had been part of Paddy Mayne's convoy of six jeeps, which made it back to base despite some hairy moments. He had been one of the lucky ones, emerging unscathed from the mission. Some of his friends had not been so fortunate. One of those lying injured back at the Wadi Gamra was Corporal Anthony Drongin, who had joined up at the same time as Chris. Although the two young men's personalities could not have been more different, they got on well. The ex-Scots Guard had once been a regimental sergeant major, but had been mysteriously stripped of his rank. He kept much to himself and gave the impression that he had some dark secret. During the shoot-out he had been in Reg Seekings' jeep and had been shot in the groin, a wound so serious that his chances of fatherhood were gone forever. As it turned out, all four of the injured men died in captivity and have no known graves to this day. It was not the outcome that Seekings would have wished for either his pal or his conscience, but he understood the harsh reality of war better than most.

The operation had been a disaster by any standards, and as if to make matters worse the attack on Tobruk had also failed miserably. About fifty men were either dead or missing from the Benghazi raid and as many vehicles had been destroyed. Among those listed as missing were 'Gentleman' Jim Almonds and his gunner, Corporal Fletcher. They had both in fact been captured during the gun battle, after their jeep had exploded. It was obvious to all that the enemy had been tipped off about the mission. According to Seekings, 'There was too much talk in Shepheards Hotel in Cairo, and places like that. Some people even felt that [it'd been] deliberately leaked, which I don't think for one minute [it] had, but it certainly appeared to the ordinary soldier that something had [been leaked]. But it was picked up from headquarters people talking out of place. We had one or two loose mouths in those days, not too bright.'

Chapter Eight

Fox on the Run

'The names come back to me as I write; and even now in imagination I can see their dark, tanned bodies, the rough, tousled hair and beards; can picture them lining up for their meal with clinking mess-tins, and can almost hear their jokes and sallies being thrown backwards and forwards. O'Dowd, Evans, Austin, Downes, Robinson, Millar, Cunningham, Shaw and many others.'

Malcolm James, Born of the Desert

When Stirling got to Cairo, he discovered that while the backroom boys at HQ were not rejoicing at the outcome of Operation Bigamy, they were certainly not putting it down as a failure. It had caused Rommel to withdraw large numbers of troops and equipment from the front line, thereby enabling the Eighth Army's counter-attack. Stirling's long meeting with Lieutenant Colonel John 'Shan' Hackett on 28 September had gone very well and he now found himself promoted to lieutenant colonel, while Paddy Mayne rose to the rank of major. The SAS also became recognized officially as a full regiment for the first time. It would be known henceforth as 1 SAS Regiment. The Regiment's structure was to be overhauled and would now comprise 29 officers and 572 men. There were to be four separate combat squadrons. Major Mayne would command A Squadron, with a new officer in charge of B Squadron, Major Vivian Street. Squadrons C and D were set up from the Free French and the SBS Folbot unit, which had originally been part of Layforce.

While their leader busied himself at HQ, his men were back at Kabrit, recuperating from their latest exertions. After a few days at Kufra they had been flown back to their base. Their lives now

91

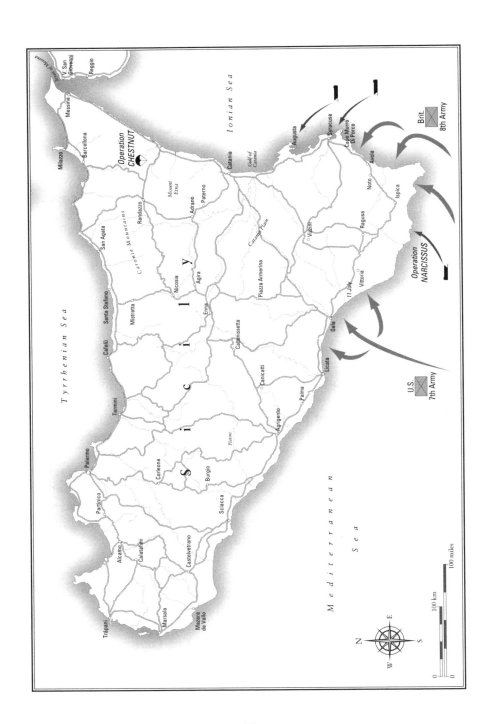

seemed to alternate between two extremes: a period of hardship, deprivation and danger in the desert, followed by a time of plenty back at Kabrit. The cold beer, regular food, and female company available in these times of leave had been the subject of their dreams for weeks. In fact Chris had more reason than most to feel pleased with himself. On 21 September he was promoted to the rank of corporal. While this was due in some degree to the further expansion of the Regiment, the courage he had shown at Benghazi had obviously not gone unnoticed.

The new corporal did not have as much time as perhaps he would have liked to celebrate around Cairo, as word soon came through that they were about to go 'up the blue' once more. Following discussions at HQ, Stirling had decided that Mayne's A Squadron would return to Kufra as soon as possible, and from there establish a fresh base on the edge of the Great Sand Sea, ready for action. He was still smarting from a terse exchange he'd had with General Montgomery, some days earlier. Monty had rounded on the SAS chief after Stirling had asked for permission to recruit from his best troops in the Eighth Army. The General considered the request 'arrogant in the extreme' and dismissed out of hand any idea of giving his best men to the young upstart. He would need every last man for his new offensive, Operation Lightfoot, which was currently at the planning stage – this would eventually conclude with the famous battle of El Alamein. So for now Stirling would have to pick his new men from the fresh troops that had recently arrived from Britain. It would take longer to bring them up to SAS standard than the more hardened veterans of the Eighth Army, but he realized there would be no shifting Montgomery.

Mayne was given his pick of the best fifty men from L Detachment, which included Chris, plus another thirty newly trained recruits from Kabrit. They left Kabrit on 7 October, arriving at Kufra six days later. At around the same time Hitler was issuing his infamous Kommandobefehl. The order was that SAS personnel were 'to be annihilated to the last man', without worrying about the inconvenient niceties of the Geneva Convention. Special units were to be set up to hunt down the raiders, able to roam freely and strike at will – they would be known as the Brandenburgers. German newspapers were now referring to Colonel Stirling as 'The Phantom Major', much to the annoyance of the Nazi propaganda people. The Regiment's first task at Kufra was to establish their winter quarters.

They built small huts from the local reeds and even ended up with a proper quartermaster's store and an officers' mess. They also set up a forward base to the north, deep in the heart of the Great Sand Sea. Howard's Cairn, as it became known, was 200 miles behind the enemy lines at El Alamein, and was both remote and inaccessible.

Life at Kufra was tolerable, apart from the swarms of flies that seemed to get everywhere. The oasis was always busy with local women and their children collecting water and washing. In the evenings the tribesmen sat in the shade of the date trees, smoking hashish and drinking coffee. They seemed bemused by all the activity, but they had become used to the comings and goings of the LRDG, who had had a base there for some time. Apart from the obvious language barrier, Mayne and his men got on well with the natives. Whether this extended as far as sharing the hashish pipe or not is not documented anywhere, but these were not men who baulked easily at the untried or unknown.

On 14 October, Major Mayne received a radio message from Cairo. The date for Montgomery's history making offensive was set for the 23rd and A Squadron were to play an integral part in the most important battle in the desert war. Their targets would no longer be the Axis airfields, however. Instead, they were to concentrate on disrupting Rommel's supply lines by destroying railways and ammunition dumps, and attacking motor transport destined for the front line. Mayne had already sent out reconnaissance patrols to identify potential targets and Bill Fraser, now his second-in-command, was at that moment leading the way on a raid. Mayne gathered seven of the remaining men, including Chris and headed for their forward base in a convoy of four jeeps. Their mission was the destruction of the coastal road and the Mersa Matruh railway line. As they crossed the wastes of the Great Sand Sea in broad daylight they became sitting ducks for any enemy planes. However, by now the RAF was gaining the upper hand in North Africa and the convoy eventually arrived safely at Howard's Cairn. The following is the Official Report of the mission:

REPORT OF JEEP OPERATION, 19TH OCTOBER, 1942.
Party: - Major Mayne, Lieut. Marsh, Moore, O'Dowd Allen, L/C. Swan.
Object: - Destruction of the railway in the area of Mersa Matruh, general nuisance raid.
Date: - Party left Howard's Cairn 19th Oct., approximately.

Result: - Mixed German and Italian convoy shot up on the Mersa Matruh-Siwa track, 20 prisoners taken, 2 only brought back, both Italian. Two trucks blown up, one shot up and abandoned (possible), one damaged. Railway track blown S.W. of Mersa Matruh in four places.

Losses: - Nil.

Execution: - The party under Major Mayne left Howard's Cairn on or around 19th October, 1942, and together with remainder of jeeps travelled through the Sand Sea to a point five miles inside the entrance, here a small advanced dump was made. The party continuing on whilst the jeeps left returned to Howard's Cairn. We travelled N.E. for a day, crossing through the boundary wire from Libya into Egypt at a point a mile south of Fort El Heria. Kept on in same direction for four or five days heading for railway South of Mersa Matruh. Lay up for a day in wadi used on one of the previous jobs, found guns and ammunition, small amount of food, but no water. O'Dowd's jeep developed axle trouble soon after setting out from this area for the target, Major Mayne sent back two jeeps to lying-up area of previous night. O'Dowd and Swan. Lt. Marsh and Moore. Major Mayne continuing on towards target was fired on by heavy M.G., rifle and 20 mm.fire. No casualties. Decided that they had hit a heavily defended area so turned back and rejoined two jeeps already sent back. O'Dowd's jeep fixed, whole party moved off the same night, to a new lying-up area. Spent three days here, trying to get news as to when the push at Alamein was to start. Unable to get through on the radio. The whole party moved off on the fourth day in easterly direction; going rough and hilly. Eighth day out at about an hour before dusk, convoy was sighted heading north along the Siwa track, about six vehicles. Major Mayne decided to attack. Two jeeps to attack the front of convoy, and halt it, other two to race for the rear. We had to chase convoy, which speeded up when it spotted us, got straddled out, so that only two-thirds of convoy was caught in pincer movement, all jeeps opened up on the convoy with K guns. Front truck going very fast got away owing to the fact that we were coming across country diagonally towards the convoy and could not reach maximum speed. Three trucks were stopped, searched, and then blown up. About twenty Italians taken prisoner, rear trucks mounted

95

M.G.s so it was decided that as convoy was not carrying anything of importance, party would move on to main target. Two prisoners were taken out of the bunch, who were all crying hard and pleading to be taken prisoner. Remainder were sent back in direction of trucks which were already going up. Party made off heading east. Learnt from prisoners that convoy was taking men from Siwa garrison to Mersa for medical attention and leave. Here, owing to a shortage of petrol and water, party split, Lt. Marsh, Moore, Swan, and O'Dowd proceeding due North to blow railway, Major Mayne with two jeeps heading back to the dump at Howard's Cairn. Lt. Marsh with two jeeps headed due north and hit railway southwest of Mersa Matruh at about 2 in the morning. Charges were fixed four on rails and two on telegraph poles. No sign of any life anywhere. Time pencils were fired and party left area heading due south; a mile from the railway O'Dowd's jeep got a puncture and neither jeep had a spare wheel ready. All four spares were U/S. The wheel had to be taken off and the puncture mended, explosions were heard.

Party moved off travelling till daybreak, reached Quarat Azza, lay up for a day, and moved off in the evening. Shortly after setting off, leading jeep ran into large shell hole, and it was obvious that the area was littered with them. Party waited for daylight before moving off, heading southwest to hit the wire before striking S.S.W. to mouth of the Sand Sea. During the morning, low-flying JU 52 sighted, and party, caught with trousers down, remained still, hoping that the plane would mistake jeeps for wrecks, many of which were lying around the area. It did. Party crossed wire, south of Fort Madalene and made for the mouth of the Sand Sea. After day's journey, although off course, party struck jeep tyre tracks, and followed them to the entrance. Chased a gazelle for ten minutes, wounded it with Ks and finished it off with pistol. Made very good eating. Arrived back at Howard's Cairn to learn that Major Mayne had had to travel for a day with both front tyres flat, owing to the fact that we had gone off with the only tyre pump in the party; he had met Capt. Fraser's party a day out from Sand Sea and got air from him. Major Mayne got back before Lt. Marsh, who was out approximately eleven or twelve days.

However the story did not quite finish there. As the patrol was returning to base and looking forward no doubt to a rest, they met a party heading out on another operation. One of their number had already been injured and Chris volunteered to take his place. The young man from Shrule was beginning to get a taste for this desert-raiding lark. The following is a brief report of the operation:

A SQUADRON, FIRST SAS REGIMENT 26TH OCTOBER.

Lt. McDermott's party left, Cpl. Sharman, Adamson, Fitch, Kerr, Gladwell, Wall and Wortley. Wortley injured and on meeting Lt. Marsh's party coming in transferred him for O'Dowd. Captured 4 M.G. posts on line south of Barrani-Bir Rim. Blew line and sidings. Trucks, food and water dumps and a Jerry signal wagon destroyed. Straffed road and got two Lancias. Losses, one jeep and one to be recovered. Returned 3rd November.

General Montgomery had launched his massive bombardment at 2140 hrs on the night of the 23rd. An hour later the big guns fell silent along the Alamein line as the infantry battle began in earnest. Meanwhile, Mayne's patrols continued to wreak havoc from their base deep inside the desert. They felt generally safe from air attacks now, as most Axis pilots considered the depths of the Great Sand Sea off-limits. Believed by many to be impassable on the ground, it was the last place a pilot wanted to crash-land. The only threat to life and limb that now remained for the SAS men were the scorpions and snakes they shared their home with. Life at the forward base was rough and ready and the desert nights grew deceptively cold at this time of year. Although they were supplied regularly from Kufra, there were no bathing facilities and with water strictly rationed, washing was out of the question. Hair and beards grew long and with many suffering from desert sores, they must have looked a terrifying bunch to any Axis soldier they happened to come upon.

Indeed this was to be one of the most successful periods for the Regiment in the whole war. The Commander was in his element. He had been given a list of the priority targets, and it was entirely at his own discretion when and how they were destroyed. While there were those in the top brass back at Cairo who must have shuddered at the thought of Paddy Mayne running riot with his own private army, they knew he was up to the job. The latest graduates from Kabrit, thrown in at the deep end, were letting nobody down. One new officer, Irishman Bill McDermott, became so frustrated when the charges failed to blow a locomotive, that he destroyed the whole station, taking the staff as prisoners. If anything, they tended to be a little too enthusiastic. There were a dodgy few moments on one occasion when Chris had laid a charge with a very short fuse. Knowing this would necessitate a speedy withdrawal, he ordered one of the new men to keep a jeep running nearby. Having lit the fuse, Chris made a bolt for the jeep. The driver, however, was a little too keen to get away and in his eagerness gave the jeep such a jolt that Chris was somersaulted off the back. Pleydell uses this incident in his book to demonstrate the difference in attitude between the Axis troops: he recounts how a group of recently taken prisoners were watching nearby and whereas the Germans saw the funny side of the mishap, he recorded that their Italian allies 'were too occupied in cowering in sheer terror to be able to appreciate it.'

With names among their number such as Kennedy, O'Reilly, Donoghue and Ward the nightly singsongs now took on a distinctly Irish flavour. The Major's love of Percy French usually meant an airing of 'Come Back Paddy Reilly' or 'The Mountains of Mourne', but often the strains of rebel songs such as 'The Foggy Dew' and 'The West's Awake' (a particular favourite of Chris's) could be heard across the shifting sand dunes, late into the night. On other occasions they would be shouted down with good-humoured banter such as 'not another bloody rebel song', while the singer retrieved a more suitable alternative from his repertoire. The objections did not come from their leader however, despite his Unionist upbringing. Malcolm James Pleydell offers the following insight in *Born of the Desert*: 'Yes, Paddy was Irish all right; Irish from top to toe; from the lazy eyes that could light into anger so quickly, to the quiet voice and its intonation. Northern Irish, mind you, and he regarded all Southerners with true native caution. But he had Southern Irishmen in his Irish patrol – they all had shamrocks painted on their jeeps – and I know he was proud of them.'

In fact, the men often joked that the Irish now seemed to be running the war in North Africa. Generals Richard O'Connor and Harold Alexander were both of Irish parenthood, Generals Cunningham and Dorman-Smith were from Dublin and Cavan respectively, while Monty was almost a neighbour of Paddy Mayne's. Even the Commander-in-Chief back in London, Sir Alan Brooke, was a County Fermanagh man. Pleydell himself was responsible for one of the new faces now in A Squadron. He had adopted a stray puppy back at Kabrit, fearing for its future, and had called it 'HMS Saunders' after the Navy base where they drank. Saunders was a small jet-black mongrel bitch who took to army life as if it was in her blood. By day she was never far away from the cookhouse, while at night she snuggled under the blankets of whichever soldier she had decided to favour on that particular evening. As the good doctor saw it: 'There was nothing snobbish about HMS Saunders! I think she slept with every man in the camp on more than one occasion.'

After ten days of ferocious battle, the Allies retook Tobruk. The Africa Korps was now in retreat and consequently A Squadron were no longer behind enemy lines. During their stay at Howard's Cairn they had blown the railway line to Tobruk no fewer than seven times. The only fatality occurred when Lieutenant Raymond Shorten was killed, when his jeep overturned while being chased by the enemy. His navigator, Trooper John Sillito, eluded the hunters and became stranded. Undaunted, this SAS novice marched the 200-odd miles back to base in eight days, with no food and one water-bottle. On 8 November, the First Army, comprising both British and American forces, landed in Algeria and soon after Mayne received orders to move shop. They would return to Kufra and from there set up a new operational base at Bir Zalten, where they would be joined by Stirling and B Squadron. Stirling had already made plans – approved by Montgomery, who seemed at last to be warming to the upstart's methods. The Regiment's new role would be to sabotage a 400-mile stretch of road running from El Agheila, where Rommel was now dug in, to Tripoli.

With the landing of the First Army to the east, the Desert Fox was now cornered and at the mercy of the Allies. Stirling decided to split each squadron into eight separate patrols. Each patrol of three jeeps would then have responsibility for a 40-mile stretch of road. A Squadron would take the eastern section from Agheila to Bourat, while B Squadron would attack the road from Bourat to Tripoli. Although he was not content with the amount of training the new men had been through – many had not done their parachute jumps, for example – he had little choice in the matter. Monty's next offensive was set for 13 December and they had to be ready.

It was with some regret that A Squadron left Howard's Cairn in mid November, but the war was moving on. It was only when they stopped for a meal some 50 miles from their old hide-out that they realized the dog, Saunders, had been left behind in all the confusion. Pleydell and some others volunteered to go back, while the rest of the Squadron waited. It took two hours to return to Howard's Cairn, where they eventually coaxed the deserter from her cover. It must have made quite a sight – a scruffy bunch of trained killers, armed to the teeth, pleading with a tiny dog to come with them. By the time they returned to the others it was almost dark and the men were bedding down for the night. According to Pleydell they 'were in little mood to appreciate either her happy barkings or the way her swishing tail nearly shook her hind legs off the ground.'

After a couple of days back at Kufra, Major Mayne and his men set off for Bir Zelten, less than 80 miles south from Rommel's lines. Once there, they busied themselves digging out hollows from the chalk caves to shelter and hide the vehicles. By the time Stirling and B Squadron arrived on 29 November, all was ready. They had left Kabrit nine days earlier in forty jeeps and a dozen lorries. This time they were able to take the coast road from Alexandria, which was strewn with burned out enemy tanks and planes. At Agedabia they turned southwest into the desert. To celebrate the reunion a party was held that night. There was even some beer to honour the occasion. It had come all the way from Kabrit and made a welcome alternative to the usual rum. The next day Stirling gathered his officers to go through the plans in detail. He explained that by concentrating on night attacks it was hoped that the enemy would have no choice but to travel by day, leaving them wide open for the RAF. Soon after, the Colonel led B Squadron to their new base at Bir Fascia, and after issuing some final instructions he left them to get on with it while he headed back to Cairo. He realized that the two Allied armies would eventually meet up and he had set his sights on the SAS being the first unit to make contact. It would, he felt, be a proper feather in the cap of the Regiment.

Back at Bir Zelten, A Squadron had sprung into action following the fresh Allied offensive on 13 December. They could hear the rumble of Monty's heavy artillery away to the north, as they huddled in their sleeping bags at night. They worried about their mates who were at that moment giving the Germans hell somewhere, their sleeping bags still rolled up. The following extract from Mayne's diary is typical of the time:

> Drove north to attack road, ran into minefield on side of road. Recced our position next morning and found ourselves west of Sirte. Skirted fort of Ksar Bou Hadi, mined road, blew telegraph poles and cratered road. The first car came along struck our mine. Later the ammonal went up with a loud explosion. Hid for three days, but now were very short of petrol and unable to get all our jeeps back. We ran one jeep on to the road as a roadblock between two trucks in a long convoy. Put mines under the wheels and filled it with our remaining explosive. The convoy stopped and, trying to pass round our jeep, hit one of our mines. Later jeep went up with terrific explosion. Drove south to hit tracks after 100 miles and returned to Bir Zelten. Much frightened by a cheetah, with whom we shared our lying-up wadi.

They had made their sleeping quarters reasonably comfortable and the sandstone caves offered them protection during the rainy periods, which were now becoming quite common. Between raids they played cards and sometimes picked up the BBC on the wireless set. It must have been a strange feeling to be gathered around the set, listening to the latest dance music being broadcast from a warm studio thousands of miles away in London. It was in these surroundings that Chris and his comrades spent Christmas and New Year's Eve 1942. They were dressed in the same clothes they had set out in six weeks earlier, as they dined on venison, the proceeds of a recent hunt, and listened to carols on the wireless. On Christmas night they held a party and sang and laughed around the campfire until the early hours. On the same day Major Street of B Squadron was captured along with his patrol.

In fact, while Mayne's men were carrying out up to sixteen successful raids per week, nothing had gone right for the new section. Inexperience, as Stirling had feared, was the main reason for the failure. In one particularly unfortunate incident a patrol came across an Italian convoy made up of three rather plush caravans. Believing that they contained some top military staff, the SAS attacked and raked the windows with the Vickers guns. When they went to inspect the damage they found to their horror that instead of Italian officers, they had killed a group of Italian prostitutes en route to some barracks. Needless to say, the men of A Squadron were blissfully unaware of this, as was Stirling who was then busy at HQ. Radio contact was now becoming unreliable and, realizing that the Eighth Army was now sweeping ahead of them, Major Mayne ordered his men to pack up.

Their war in the desert was over and it was time to return to Kabrit. The journey took them through Tobruk and along the coastal road through Hell Fire Pass and El Alamein itself, to Mersa Mutruh. To the north was the Mediterranean Sea while, on their southern flank, the wreckage of the battle lay strewn across the desert floor for miles. The Afrika Korps were now making a beeline for Tunisia, from where their commander would resign due to ill health within six weeks. By May 250,000 Germans had surrendered and the Allies had dealt Hitler a devastating blow. El Alamein was their first decisive victory and a major turning point in the war. It prompted Churchill to voice his cautious opinion, 'This is not the end, or even the beginning of the end, but it is perhaps the end of the beginning.' The band of unkempt, scruffy, and war-weary men presently returning to base had helped in no small way towards this achievement. During the course of the North African campaign the SAS had destroyed over 400 enemy aircraft. Since September 1942, A Squadron had carried out forty-three successful raids on key enemy positions and communications, and had blown the railway line seven times. Now they wanted nothing more than a wash, clean clothes, some cold beer and a warm bed.

Chapter Nine

New Name and New Leader

The men of A Squadron were delighted to hear that they were soon to be granted a spell of leave. Montgomery had already congratulated Stirling on their contribution, and to demonstrate his appreciation he had invited Commander-in-Chief General Alexander to visit Kabrit. Stirling missed the visit, as he had gone to check on B Squadron's situation. On 14 January, Alexander was treated to a demonstration in explosives and firepower, and seemed suitably impressed with the most unorthodox regiment ever likely to come under his command. With the top brass out of the way, it was time to prepare for some long-overdue leave. Bill Deakins was a Canadian-born Royal Engineer corporal who had joined up at the same time as Chris. Despite their differing backgrounds, they got on well enough to take the fortnight's leave together. Deakins came from an affluent family and was public school educated, but class structures counted for little in the SAS. He was two years older than his friend, but as an engineer he was not as battle-hardened and had spent much of his time at Kabrit. Fortunately for the purposes of this narrative, towards the end of his life Deakins published his war memoirs. His book, *The Lame One: Sod This for a Game of Soldiers*, contains a tantalizing, if somewhat vague, account of their adventures over the fourteen days in 'Civvy Street'.

While his pal may have been the senior, reading between the lines it would seem that Chris was the more 'street wise' of the two. They picked a reasonably priced hotel in Cairo for the first week's vacation. It was cool and airy and close to all their favourite hotspots. They had plenty of pay to spend and their kitbags were already stuffed with hundreds of cigarettes. The cigarettes had been sent by family and friends and were waiting for them when they returned to Kabrit. They were now wearing well-fitting uniforms and looked very smart in their battledress, blue shirts, ties and dark-blue side hats. They were proud of their distinctive uniforms but they disclosed little information about their Regiment. In fact, many who saw their SAS shoulder flashes took them as being from the South African services.

The city was much quieter by now, as the soldiers who had thronged its streets for the last few years were now busy laying their lives on the line many hundreds of miles away. The two men enjoyed sipping beers outside a bar, while they watched the world go by. Deakins describes 'watching simple things such as the traffic on the river, the overloaded and ramshackle lorries bringing the country produce to the city, donkey or oxen carts carrying the baggage of peasant families. Females with heavy loads on their heads, following their male counterpart some paces ahead. The bazaars and souvenir shops, anything to take money, the pimps offering the delights of a sister, many areas out of bounds no doubt for a serviceman's own protection, more especially if they had been drinking.' They avoided what could have been a nasty incident when Deakins responded to a very insistent shoeshine boy by treading on his fingers. His patience had finally worn out after the pair had been pestered continuously. The lad screamed in exaggerated pain, and in an instant a crowd of men had sprung from the back streets to avenge his injury. 'Discretion being the better part of valour,' he wrote, 'SAS or not, we were fortunate to beat a hasty retreat on a passing bus.'

Later on they ventured into the notorious brothel area of Sharia El Birka, although Deakins insists they did not sample the delights therein: 'I was not a prude about sex, but paying for pleasure had no attraction for me, more especially when one saw the queues that were waiting to share a limited number of girls.' In fact Churchill had recently threatened to shut the place down, believing it to be the cause of the high rate of venereal disease amongst his soldiers. The troops were supplied with tins of disinfectant to prevent disease, but it wasn't always effective. Eventually the two young men engaged one of the girls in chat for a while. When they asked what she planned to do when the place closed down, she informed them she was going to marry her man and start a family in the country. The two pals wished her well and moved on. Continuing in their quest for romance, they eventually got to know two Italian-Egyptian girls in a bar and spent the evening with them. Later the couples took a horse-drawn carriage ride along the moonlit Nile. The author

104

avoids detail at this point except to offer the advice that 'whatever the precautions, sex in a horse-drawn trap is no success.'

After a week of this blatant decadence, the friends decided to head for Alexandria. They were already familiar with the streets of the great capital, whereas Alexandria would be a fresh experience. They spent the days wandering up and down the seafront, where they took photographs and lounged around the bars and restaurants. They relished the sea breezes and the lush vegetation. Here, there were not so many bazaars and fewer pimps and touts to pester them. 'For the experience', they paid a visit to the red-light district of Sister Street. Here also they found differences with Cairo. Exhibitionism appeared to be the speciality of the district and there was much to keep the voyeur intrigued. Deakins describes, 'Enlarged photographs of such things as a girl taking a donkey, positions and postures. A girl, there and then in the room, showing how she could take a half pint beer bottle up inside her, watched by maybe six or eight men in the room. Another girl demonstrated how she could pick up large coins in her vagina, that is until, unbeknown to her, someone had heated a large coin with lit matches, placing it on the edge of the table.' Pandemonium followed the unfortunate girl's screams and once more, a hasty retreat was called for. The days flew by and it was soon time to haggle for a few last minute souvenirs and postcards. Then they took the train back to Cairo where they met up with the leave truck for the return to Kabrit.

They soon came back down to earth on hearing the news that their commander had been captured. He had been missing almost from the time that the men of A Squadron had gone to Lebanon, although his capture was not officially verified until St Valentine's Day. Stirling had gone to join the remainder of B Squadron and found that of the original officers only three remained, the rest having been killed or captured. His plan had been to drive to Tunisia and be the first of Montgomery's troops to make contact with the First Army. Such a feat would undoubtedly be a scoop for the regiment. But on 23 January, as they approached Tunisia, his group ran into a German armoured reconnaissance unit and, after a brief skirmish Stirling was 'in the bag'. Soon after Rommel wrote to his wife with the good news: 'During January, a number of our AA gunners [sic] succeeded in surprising a British column ... and captured the commander of 1 SAS Regiment, Lt. Col. David Stirling ... Thus the British lost the very able and adaptable commander of the desert group which had caused us more damage than any other British unit of equal size.'

However three members of the patrol, including Johnny Cooper, evaded capture and some days later they made it to the front line. They got a cool reception from the suspicious Americans and were kept under armed guard until their credentials were checked out. Word soon spread among the various press correspondents, who were waiting to pounce on the SAS men. The shock was visible on the faces of the reporters when the trio emerged, looking more like a bunch of tramps than advancing British soldiers.

There was also bad news of a personal nature for Major Mayne. His father had died suddenly on 11 January, but his application for compassionate leave had been turned down. Naturally, the Major was devastated by the refusal, and it is at this point that one of the myths surrounding Mayne was born. According to many early accounts Mayne, crazed with drink, went hunting for the BBC correspondent, Richard Dimbleby, around the hotels of Cairo. Apparently the Ulsterman believed Dimbleby had a cheek reporting battle scenes from the safety of a hotel lounge and he intended letting him know. Disappointed at not locating his prey, he proceeded to wreck several hotels before being restrained, arrested, and promptly freed once more. As Hamish Ross points out in *Paddy Mayne*, Dimbleby was far away in London at this stage and had been for several months.

Whatever the truth, HQ had more important things to deal with now, such as how to best employ the SAS going forward. With their leader captured, there were the usual murmurs of impending disbandment. While there would have been support from 'the enemy within' for such a decision, it would hardly have got past Montgomery. Although the latest news from Stalingrad was encouraging, there was a perceived threat of a German advance in the Caucasus. Should it happen, the Allies would need to slow their progress by occupying and holding the mountainous regions of Turkey, Iraq and what was then Persia. With some special training, the SAS would be ideal for the role. Consequently, following a regimental party and concert, the men of A Squadron set out on a new adventure.

On 24 January, Major Mayne, along with sixty-five officers and men and Saunders the dog, set off for the little village of Berchaire, high up amongst the cedars of Lebanon. The Middle East Ski School would be their home for the next few weeks. Among the officers was the redoubtable Bob Melot, now recovered from his injuries at Benghazi. Melot's language skills would be much in demand at the school. The entire party flew to Beirut, from where they set out for the snow-capped mountains. After a three-hour drive, mostly uphill, they arrived at the school and settled in. The contrast between the desert and their new surroundings could not have been starker. For Chris, it must have evoked memories of the Norwegian fjords, and those early days of the Irish Guards. But all that must have seemed a lifetime away by now. The scenery was breathtaking. Groves of cedar trees were spread out over the mountains – some of them, according to legend, had been planted during the reign of King Solomon. Days on the ski-slopes were followed by evenings spent around the fire playing cards and drinking arak, the local wine. Sharp sand was replaced by soft snow and any desert sores the men had had soon cleared up in the cold mountain air.

After a couple of weeks Mayne was suddenly summoned back to Cairo, and he left the men to crack on with it. The future of the Regiment was now at stake and Paddy would need all his wits about him. Unlike in the desert, his enemies at HQ were invisible and they plotted in secrecy. While some grudgingly tolerated Stirling, he was, at least, one of their own. Handing control of a misfit regiment like the SAS to the fiery Irishman was certainly not in the script. Already, in his absence, command of 1 SAS had been given to Lieutenant Colonel Henry 'Kid' Cator of the Royal Scots Greys. But if they expected Mayne to stammer incoherently and storm out of the meeting in a temper, they were very much mistaken. Blair 'Paddy' Mayne may not have been upper class, but he was university educated and could debate rationally with the best of them. It would be foolhardy, he argued, to disband such a highly trained force capable of operating behind enemy lines, when the war was yet to be decided. Mayne fought long and hard to retain the unit, and eventually won his superiors round. However the unit was stripped of its regimental status and was renamed the Special Raiding Squadron. However, while Cator would remain in overall command on paper, he would have little say in procedures in future.

Meanwhile, the threat from the Caucasus had dissipated following the Russian success at Stalingrad, and the men were immediately called back from Lebanon. The war was now turning back towards Europe and it was clear that the SAS could not operate there using the same methods as it had in the desert. While its future destination was kept top secret, the unit was now to undergo training in assault landings and cliff scaling.

Mayne finished the negotiations and on 19 March returned to Kabrit, where he assembled the troops, including those just back from the ski-school. There were a few well-suppressed groans when he announced that they were to embark on a new intensive re-training programme, in preparation for their next mission. Mayne was a stickler for fitness and while Chris and his mates in A Squadron had proved themselves repeatedly, none of the latest recruits had ever done Commando training. On an organizational level, 1 SAS was to be divided into two groups: 1 Special Raiding Squadron (SRS) under Mayne, and 1 Special Boat Section (SBS) under George Jellicoe. The SRS (about 280, including all ranks) would come from Chris's A Squadron, the survivors of B Squadron and some new recruits. They were divided into Nos 1, 2 and 3 Troops, under Bill Fraser, Harry Poat and a new man, Captain David Barnby respectively. As was the case in the Commandos, each squadron leader got to pick his own men and Bill Fraser chose Chris for No. 1 Troop. Fraser's Troop was considered the most elite, as it contained most of the hardened veterans from the desert war. Troops 2 and 3 had had little or no fighting experience so far. The men were relieved to learn the unit now had a future and a fresh goal, and there were loud cheers when Mayne finished his talk. A little later Chris was told of his change in rank. He was now Lance Sergeant O'Dowd, his second promotion in less than a year. That evening there was much cause for celebration and the mess was busy. Some, like Malcolm Pleydell, had decided to cash in their chips and leave the unit. Mike Sadler was going to complete his long-postponed parachute training at another base. Sadler had been with Stirling's party when the leader was captured, but had escaped along with Johnny Cooper, who was already away on officer train-ing. Bill Fraser had just recently returned from Tunisia, where he had been involved in some hush-hush job. It was a rare chance for old comrades to catch up on recent exploits and recall past ones, to share a song and a drink while the opportunity presented itself.

An advance party left the next day to prepare their new training base in Palestine. The main body of the new Squadron travelled by train through El Qantara, El Arish, Gaza and the Strip before finally arriving at Az Zib, a small coastal village near the Syrian border on 25 March. The base consisted of a few huts for storing supplies and a ramshackle cinema, while the men would make do with sleeping in tents. They were flanked on one side by the Mediterranean Sea; on the other side they could make out the Syrian mountains. There was a camp of Palestinian families close by, who kept sheep and goats. Mayne set about his task with his usual gusto. For old hands like Chris, there would be many changes to contend with. The days of terrifying enemy guards in jeeps mounted with twin Vickers were over. From now, they would have to carry their weapons on foot. The .303 calibre Bren gun soon became the weapon of choice, as the men tested and vetoed the alternatives. Although the Bren could only fire off a maximum of 500 rounds per minute, it was accurate and extremely reliable. They also became familiar with their enemy's weapons, in case they were needed to get out of a jam. For a final polish, the men were sent in sections to a shooting range in Jerusalem for pistol practice.

Captain Bill Cumper and his team instructed the new men in the use of explosives, particularly the Lewes bomb. A mortar platoon was formed and put under the command of Lieutenant Alex Muirhead. Despite the men having no experience of mortars whatsoever, Muirhead soon licked them into shape. A local beach, south of their base camp, was chosen for training in assault landing and cliff climbing. Here they learned to use rope ladders and familiarized themselves with the climbing equipment, until the routines became second nature. After successfully negotiating the cliffs with the new equipment, they then learned to climb using only their bare hands. When all that was accomplished they repeated the exercises by night, carrying their weapons and equipment and using the landing craft. In order to reach peak fitness, Mayne and his men went on gruelling route marches of up to 48 miles at a time, carrying the minimum water supply and up to 60 lbs of equipment each. All this was done in daytime temperatures that rarely fell below 100 degrees Fahrenheit. He was determined to sort the wheat from the chaff and no one, including officers, was exempt from his rigorous regime.

Inevitably, the drop-out rates were high. Some men couldn't take the heat and suffered badly with dehydration. Others were unable to take the sheer physical pain their bodies suffered and just gave up. Lieutenant Colonel Mayne, as he now was, RTU'd the weak links immediately. Some officers felt he was a little too eager to get rid of men who had at least had the courage to volunteer for the SAS, but Mayne was adamant. He had also sacked men in the past for using bad language. Mayne was not a prude and understood only too well that men liked to curse and swear when excited, or under pressure. However, he couldn't abide the use of bad language in everyday conversation and came down heavily on anyone who used it. The men relished whatever leave time they managed and in the evenings they walked to Nahariya, where there was a fine beach and several cafes and bars.

On 13 May they received a visit from Lieutenant General Miles Dempsey, Commander of XIII Corps, Eighth Army. The war in North Africa had been officially declared over on the previous day. Dempsey watched the men carry out a mock assault on a pillbox, having first scaled the towering cliffs with the minimum of fuss. He was impressed with the display laid on for him and told them so. Soon, he promised, they would take part in an all-out attack on southern Europe, landing in Sicily. In fact Combined Operations, under the command of Admiral Lord Louis Mountbatten, had mooted plans for invading Sicily as far back as January, when it was felt that the month of July would afford the best moonlight for a landing. While Churchill believed the island to be 'the soft under-belly of Europe', he also knew the Axis were likely to be expecting them. In order to put them off the scent, an elaborate deception, codenamed Operation Mincemeat, was put in motion. This involved releasing a man's body from a submarine, so that it would wash up on the Spanish mainland. The body was dressed in the uniform of a Royal Marine major, and carried papers that suggested plans for an imminent attack on northern Italy.

The real attack, codenamed Husky, would present its own problems. Sicily was heavily fortified, with two German and at least ten Italian divisions based there. The island also had several airfields and four major ports. Husky would be the largest amphibious invasion of the war to date and it would comprise the American Seventh Army and the British Eighth Army. The plan was to take the southeast corner and capture the port of Siracusa (Syracuse) as soon as possible. The Special Raiding Squad were tasked with capturing and destroying the coastal batteries at Capo Murro di Porco, a headland south of Siracusa. 'Subsequent action', according to General Dempsey's final orders, was 'at the discretion of

OC Squadron.' His visit had convinced him of the squadron's worth and he felt their commander would revel in the added responsibility. For now, the name of their exact target and date would be kept secret, but the men knew enough to whet their appetite. The six-week slog they had just come through would not be in vain, and Sicily sounded as good a place to start a scrap as the next.

At the end of the General's visit his attention was drawn to one particular soldier who looked very young. Private 'Titch' Davison had already lost three brothers to the war before he himself enlisted in the Durham Light Infantry at the age of fifteen, only two years earlier. Davison was called forward and asked his age. 'Twenty-one, sir,' was the prompt reply. Dempsey said: 'No, your real age.' Davison stuck to his guns: 'Twenty-one, sir.' 'No, no, no,' replied the General, 'I'm not going to do anything to you, I just out of curiosity want to know your proper age.' 'Twenty-one sir, and if you don't fucking like it, you can stuff it!' Dempsey just laughed and said: 'I wish I had two or three divisions like him. Keep an eye on him, sergeant major.' After the General took his leave, Mayne and his men pored over the aerial maps and sketches he had left for their benefit. They soon built a replica of their future target at Capo Murro de Porco and practised the raid until it became second nature.

On the morning of 6 June, the Squadron left Az Zib for Suez. They were seen off by their Palestinian neighbours, who would now have further to walk for their water. As they drove up to Suez, they couldn't but have been impressed by the massive armada that was moored in the docks. They were soon being ferried out, along with their equipment, to the *Ulster Monarch*, an ex-passenger ferry that had sailed between Belfast and Liverpool in better times. Once aboard, the men slung their hammocks in the mess decks and went on an inspection tour of their new home. There was much rejoicing when an amply stocked bar was discovered between the decks.

By the morning they were cruising down the Red Sea to the Gulf of Aqaba. Here they would spend the next three weeks perfecting the skills of assault landings. They were provided with eight LCAs (Landing Craft Assault) which were 40 feet in length and capable of carrying up to thirty-five men. With the LCAs drawn alongside the ship, they practised climbing up and down the rope ladders for days on end. They mounted attack after attack on the local beaches, learning to evacuate the flat-bottomed assault craft and crawl up the beach with speed. While all this was done in sweltering temperatures and calm seas, it was decided to give the men a taste of what their mission would be like in less favourable weather conditions. They were towed by the *Ulster Monarch* at top speed for up to an hour at a time, while the seaspray poured into the LCAs and drenched the passengers. Navy issue tots of rum were given out to the frozen men once they were back on board. Most of Fraser's 1 Troop, including Chris, had acquired their sea legs with the Commandos, and could take whatever the sea could throw at them. The other troops were lacking such experience however, and it showed. They suffered greatly from seasickness, which led in turn to a lot of micky-taking by the old sea dogs of 1 Troop.

They were back in Suez by the end of June. The armada had increased during their absence, and the docks were thronged with troops loading equipment on the quayside. The men were now confined to ship and were kept busy with boat drills and weapon inspections. At night they could see the inviting lights of the Suez bars, where they had spent wild times in the recent past. The issue of the Squadron's new uniform helped to break this brief spell of monotony. Gone were the days of Arab headdresses and camouflage jackets, which had so often saved their bacon in the desert. They now wore a type of tam o'shanter with an SAS badge of brass, blue flannel shirts, black lanyards, khaki drill trousers with crepe-soled boots and white socks. The camouflage had served them well 'up the blue' but the new uniform emphasized their changed role in the war – as storm troopers, they would need to be distinguishable from the enemy, to minimize the risk of friendly fire. Once more, they vetoed the wearing of steel helmets on several grounds. They could be noisy and they were relatively heavy. More especially, the men had a theory that if a man was relying on that sort of protection, which only covered one part of the body, his mind would be less focused on the job at hand.

They soon had an opportunity to show off their new clobber when General Montgomery paid a visit on 28 June. The men had mixed feelings about Monty, with some finding him arrogant on occasion. Many resented the fact that he had replaced the more popular Auchinleck, who had always been a good friend to the Regiment. Montgomery was given command when better equipment and extra troops had been provided, which had made his job a lot easier. He congratulated the men on their desert triumphs and their high fitness levels. He told his audience they were to be the advance guard of the new operation and gave them the challenger password. 'The challenge is "Desert Rats",' he said, 'and the password is "Kill the Italians", and that's exactly what I want you to do.' It had been decided beforehand not to give Montgomery the customary 'three cheers' until the very last moment, and the strategy caused the General to depart in some confusion. As he backed uncertainly up the companionway he was heard to mutter, 'wonderful discipline, wonderful discipline! Very smart. I like their hats.' On 1 July, the Special Raiding Squadron with an overall strength of eighteen officers and 262 other ranks, boarded the *Monarch* and sailed to Port Said, where they spent a further three days making last minute adjustments and fine-tuning the plans.

On 5 July they sailed out as part of the huge invasion force of almost 500,000 men. The convoy contained over 2,300 ships of all types while 4,000 aircraft would supply air cover. As a minesweeper began to clear a channel ahead, the weather could not have been better. Spirits were high among the men as they watched the ship's crew go to work. It was going to be a stiff test for the new men who had yet to see action. For Chris and the other seasoned campaigners, it was also a turning point. They were leaving a theatre of war in which they had enjoyed much success. The principles of their founder, who was a prisoner in Colditz by this stage, had been sacrificed once again, and the Squadron was reverting back to the old Commando style raids. Nevertheless, David Stirling would have been pleased if he could have seen them from his castle prison cell. He had already indicated his wish for Mayne to succeed him, in smuggled messages to HQ, and the fact that his second-in-command had trained the men to the limits of their endurance was certain to count in their favour.

Chapter Ten

'Like terriers after rats'

Before we came on this op., we were inspected and spoken to
by all the generals and, I believe, impressed them with our
looks and turnout. I was pleased about that, but I was more
pleased by the way we impressed the Jerries and Eyeties, and
we did that to no mean tune. We went at them like terriers
after rats.

Blair 'Paddy' Mayne in a letter to his sister, Barbara

By the time the SRS arrived off the Sicilian coast, at 1930 hrs on
9 July, the weather conditions had worsened considerably. The
overall plan was for the Eighth Army to land on the southeast of the
island at Pachino, while the US 7th Army would land to the southwest at Gela. Prior to the landings, paratroops were to be flown in by
glider, but now as they approached the island, the men of the SRS
could already see the calamity in the waters ahead. Most of the
gliders had been blown off course or had fallen short of their target.
Their wreckage was now strewn across the seashore as the blacked-
out armada neared its target. The Squadron's mission was to spearhead the attack of General Dempsey's Eighth Army on its right
flank, by taking out the guns at Capo Murro di Porco. All along the
coast similar assault troops, such as the recently formed Royal
Marine Commandos, would be leading their own attacks. They had
spent the last few days cruising the Mediterranean in ideal weather
conditions. They played gin rummy, sipped beer and put on every
gramophone record in the captain's ample collection. They had seen
the tip of Mount Etna in the distance as they lounged on deck
listening to the Glen Miller band on the ship's tannoy. Now the
waiting was over, and shortly after midnight on 10 July, the same
tannoy barked out the order, 'Get Prepared and Take up Stations.'

115

The gale was now reaching force seven and the *Monarch* rolled and lurched in protest. Despite a few near disasters the men managed to board the LCAs and immediately sped towards the shore. The only sounds that were audible over the gale were their own engines and the occasional drone of an RAF bomber. As the nine boats drew nearer to the wreckage they could see survivors hanging on for their lives. Their hopes had been raised when they heard the approach of the LCAs, but they were to be quickly disappointed. As Chris and his mates sped by they heard the pleadings of the desperate, and were powerless to help. They were already behind schedule and the Eighth Army was counting on them. Once again Reg Seekings, as acting leader of Chris's A Section, found himself in a familiar unenviable position: 'We shouted to them to hang on, but we couldn't stop to pick them up, we had to go in. We were called a few names for that, but we'd got an operation. People might find it hard to understand these days, but my first objective is to get there. I've got batteries to destroy.' Already, they could make out the outline of four gun emplacements, perched menacingly on top of the cliffs. The RAF had silenced them for the moment, but their gunners were still bound to be nearby, waiting for the heat to die down.

The Squadron landed without mishap and the men were surprised to find the beach had not been mined. They met no resistance until they had scaled the cliff, when the Italians opened up with tracer fire from several directions. Much of it was coming from a nearby farmhouse and Mayne directed 3 Troop to take it out. He himself, along with the rest of the men, would deal with the batteries. The Commander had anticipated the likelihood of close combat in the assault, and before they went in he gave the order to fix bayonets. For Chris, this was a throwback to his days with the Micks and the last time anyone had used a bayonet was in the Commandos. As a lance sergeant, he was now in charge of his own sub-section of four men. No. 1 Troop was now under the command of Johnny Wiseman, a young officer who had joined the fray at the same time as Chris, with Reg Seekings as his number two. Bill Fraser had been injured and was recovering in hospital. The sections attacked from different angles and soon overran the defences. They found the survivors hiding in their underground bunkers, in no mood to fight. The sight of sharp steel had been too much for them and they had abandoned the comrades who now lay dead or wounded above them. Meanwhile, the men of 3 Troop took control of the farmhouse in similar fashion and the guns were soon silenced. The Sappers, led by Sergeant Bill Deakins, lost no time in blowing up the guns and at 0500 hrs Paddy Mayne fired off the green Very light to signal the coast was now clear. He then ordered the men and prisoners to head for the farmhouse where they could take stock.

As soon as they arrived, two more batteries situated a further 5 miles inland opened up on the ships. Realizing the situation called for immediate action, Mayne prepared his men to launch another attack. They were now responsible for over fifty prisoners and could not afford to waste manpower guarding them. Luckily, however, along with the prisoners, they had also come across several survivors of the glider assault who were fit enough to act as guards. The armada's big guns were now returning fire with interest, but several shells were falling dangerously short of the target. Realizing this would be a hindrance to his men, Mayne sent a radio message to halt the barrage until further notice. As the Squadron made its way towards the targets, the men came under constant attack from the various farmhouses en route. As one section approached a building, the occupants emerged with their hands raised while frantically weaving a white flag. But as the SRS men moved in to search them, one of the group suddenly produced a machine gun and opened up on the section. Several men were hit, but Corporal Geoff Caton took the full force of the round and died sometime later. Needless to say, his killer and many of his companions had already suffered the same fate. The Squadron was being fired on from several directions by now. There were a number of pillboxes dotted around the hills, and sniper fire was a constant threat to their progress. As they advanced, the various sections pinpointed their specific targets and wiped out the resistance.

By early afternoon the fighting was over. At that point the Squadron had gathered another 400 prisoners, while a further 200 of the enemy lay dead or wounded. They had also rescued more of the airborne troops who had been captured after landing. The SRS had lost only one man, Corporal Caton, with two injured. They had destroyed eighteen large guns and four mortars during the attack. The first thing on the men's minds now was food, which was understandable given the energy they had just expended. The food store was quickly found and plundered. After enjoying a leisurely breakfast the Squadron and its prisoners set off on the main road to the port of Syracuse. Arriving there, they met up with the forward elements of the British 5th Division who happily relieved them of their prisoners. Delighted to be free of the responsibility, the men made themselves comfortable for the night. Next morning, they marched to the harbour where the *Monarch* stood at anchor. They were looking forward to a brief rest after their recent exertions, but HQ had other ideas. No sooner were they back on the mother ship and beginning to come down from the adrenaline high, than word went round that Mayne had received fresh and urgent orders.

Mayne and his senior officers had very little time to study the maps and aerial photographs he had just received. The operation would be similar to the one they had just successfully completed, with one noticeable difference – it would be carried out in broad daylight. The orders were to capture and hold the Italian naval base at Augusta.

'We were pretty well knackered after the march into Syracuse and we were all relaxing,' remembers Bob Bennett, a Londoner who had been one of the first of Stirling's recruits. 'Then that afternoon, over the blower comes word that we have to do another landing, right away, but not to worry because it was only a mopping-up operation. Only half the usual rations and ammo. We began to think of it as a piece of cake.' They were to have a rude awakening however. Intelligence reports had already indicated the presence of crack German troops in the port, in support of the Italians. This, in turn, gave weight to the theory that Augusta was being used as a sub-marine base from which to attack the Allied shipping convoys. The *Ulster Monarch* erupted in a busy frenzy as the men drew the necessary provisions and rearmed, ready to enter the fray once more.

On 12 July at 1930 hrs, the first wave of LCAs were launched in ideal summer weather. Mayne decided to let 3 Troop take the lead, while the rest of the Squadron would follow shortly after. By now the *Monarch* had cruised to within 300 yards of the shore and the enemy's big guns responded accordingly. However, luckily for all concerned, the British cruiser, HMS *Norfolk*, with an escort of three destroyers, happened to be in the area and was in radio contact with the *Ulster Monarch*. They soon replied with interest and one by one the enemy guns were destroyed. The *Monarch* had got in on the act and was busy pounding the defences with her 20 mm cannons. Meanwhile, the LCAs were attracting a hail of machine gun from all sides as they sped towards the shore. As soon as they landed, they began to return fire. Several of the assault craft had been mounted with Vickers K guns that had been salvaged from the North African campaign. The guns they had come to depend on in the desert had lost none of their effectiveness, and they gave the men an opportunity to find some cover. As Chris watched with his mates on the deck of the *Monarch*, he knew he would soon have to make a similar journey. For now, all they could do was watch helplessly as their comrades did their utmost to resist the fierce onslaught.

It was now evident to Mayne that the intelligence reports had been accurate, and that the port was indeed well defended. There were also dozens of pillboxes sited in the hills overlooking the town. What he didn't know was that the defenders included a large section of the notoriously tough Hermann Goering Panzer Division. It was most certainly not going to be 'a piece of cake', as Bob Bennett had earlier assumed. Protected by the onslaught from the Vickers, 3 Troop picked their way along the shore and made it over the sea wall. So far they had escaped lightly, having only lost two of the medical team during the gunfight. From there they began to infiltrate the town, while the LCAs landed the rest of the Squadron without further serious mishap. Closing in on the town the Squadron split into its various sections, and the men began the dangerous job of clearing the streets, house by house. As they probed deeper the resistance became more ferocious. 'We went down both sides of a street with each group covering the buildings on the other side,' Bennett remembered, 'with a "Black Charlie" of each section walking backwards to cover the rear. If a building was occupied we used grenades. You threw a couple in, then smashed through the door spraying the room with fire as you went. We killed quite a few that way and there weren't many prisoners.'

When dusk fell the Squadron had cleared the town of enemy resistance and began to set up its defensive positions. By now they were running dangerously short of ammunition, having left the ship in the belief they were heading for a mere 'mopping up' job. After a relatively peaceful night, the men awoke to hear that elements of the 17th Brigade were approaching the town to relieve them and to help repel any counter-attack. The SRS men were delighted to hand over control of the situation; they would, at last, have a chance to let their hair down and relax. They had spent the last three days in the heat of battle and all had cheated death on many occasions. A group of men had been detailed to bury their only casualties, the medical

119

orderlies Corporal John Bentley and Private George Shaw. When their fallen comrades had been afforded the dignity they deserved, the party began in earnest. Wine and champagne flowed in abundance as the men let off steam in the morning sun. Second on their list of priorities was food. The men had had little to eat in three days and had left behind a first-rate meal on their mother ship to take on this job. Some had sustained themselves by picking the tomatoes, peaches and almonds that grew in abundance everywhere, but now the smell of food cooking on campfires filled the air. Some who had found the going to be particularly tough, spent their time relaxing in the shade and reflecting on what they had just come through. But for the majority of the men, it was party time.

An impromptu concert soon broke out with all the usual songs being sung. The highlight of the show was when Private Kit Kennedy, resplendent in a top hat, took over the musical duties by playing a pianola in the middle of the street. Waltzing around him were his mates, dragged up in women's clothes they had plundered from an abandoned brothel. A group of war correspondents who had been filming the landings had arrived on the scene and could hardly believe their eyes. This was not how they had pictured the men of the SAS – dancing, drunk on the streets, dressed in bras, French knickers, stockings, suspenders and high-heeled shoes. Paddy Mayne paid them little heed. He was never a stickler for petty rules and strongly believed that any good soldier deserved 'the spoils of war'. In fact he had already enlisted the expertise of Bill Deakins to help him blow up a couple of safes that he had come across. The results were disappointing and Mayne gave the jewellery items they had found to his sergeant. As the high jinks continued, an army provost marshal appeared on the scene with the intention of bringing the area under military rule. He dispatched a rather pompous captain to meet Colonel Mayne, with a view to halting the looting. The encounter was not to his liking, however. He left the building a lot quicker than he had entered, and felt rather fortunate to be leaving by the door. The hapless young man was unaware of two things – Mayne's determination to stand by his men no matter what, and his deep-seated hatred of the Red Caps. His Squadron had just captured the first major Axis harbour in Europe in broad daylight, and had not seen a civilian since then. Besides, the locals had long abandoned whatever items they were now picking up.

Later that evening, the men made their way to the harbour where a Greek destroyer was waiting to return them to the *Monarch.* Arriving as they did, loaded down with bottles of wine, typewriters, bicycles and clothes, and with no uniforms to speak of, many of the sailors mistook them for a group of Italian refugees. Nevertheless, a heroes' welcome awaited them on the mother ship. The showers had been prepared and a slap-up meal was all but ready. The purser was delighted with his new typewriter and deals were being struck all over the ship. Even the pianola made it back on board, where it was to hold pride of place in the ship's lounge until the *Monarch* went out of service, many years later. Although they didn't know it yet, the Squadron had seen its last action in Sicily. Operations on the island had been expected to last about three months. In fact, they lasted a little longer than five weeks, and by 10 August, Sicily had fallen. Attention was now turning to the invasion of the Italian mainland.

On board the *Monarch*, the men had every reason to feel satisfied. Both operations had been brilliantly executed. At Capo Murro di Porco they had destroyed three coastal defence and three anti-aircraft guns as well as a range finder and several heavy machine guns. They had captured Augusta in broad daylight before the enemy could destroy the valuable equipment and stores it held. They had killed or wounded hundreds of the enemy, while only losing three of their own friends. Ten of the Squadron had been injured in the process. The following report appeared in a German newspaper:

> We had suffered absolute hell from the Royal Air Force bombing and from the accuracy of the naval shelling, but it was the last straw when in daylight a British Parachute Regiment (the S.R.S.) landed at Augusta. We were helpless, machine guns, artillery and mortars were turned on them but they still came on, nothing could stop them.

The Squadron's stay on board the *Monarch* was a brief one, and a couple of days later the men were ordered to collect their gear and kitbags, and prepare for disembarkation. The ship was being dispatched back to the Middle East, while the SRS would have to make do with a temporary camp near Augusta. It was a sad parting for all concerned, and served to demonstrate how impersonal war could actually be. Their new base stood on an olive-covered plain over-looking the town and harbour they had recently captured. It was a big comedown from the shipboard luxury they had grown used to, but they had been well accustomed to rough living in the past. During this brief and uneventful time several operations were planned, only to be cancelled sometime later. For veterans like Chris, it was an unpleasant reminder of their early Commando days, but the Allied advance was such that the planners were now struggling to keep up.

After several weeks Mayne received orders to move camp once more. This time they took a train further north along the Sicilian coast to Cannizzaro, near Catania. Here conditions were much better. Their headquarters turned out to be the local doctor's house, while the men camped in the huge garden. The new camp also boasted a NAAFI and a post office of sorts. The men were glad to hear from home, when the backlog of mail arrived from Kabrit. Rations had also improved and as they were now being paid regularly once more, they could augment their diet with local bread, fruit, chicken and pork. There was a memorable incident involving the squadron padre, Captain Lunt, during their stay. He had been looking after the spiritual needs of his flock by holding an open-air service, when a German Messerschmitt fighter plane approached. The padre, deep in concentration, completely failed to notice the familiar drone, even as his congregation scattered for the nearest cover. At last looking up from his prayer book, he quickly realized the danger and joined his flock in the bushes, just in the nick of time.

One day was spent climbing Mount Etna, after Mayne had decided they needed a change from gin rummy. The entire Squad-ron, including the rather irate cooks, were ordered to ascend the 11,000 feet to the summit. Only the sick and wounded were exempt from the climb and even they had to be officially excused by the medical officer, Captain Phil Gunn. Having reached the summit, the men decided to celebrate their achievement by opening the bottles they had carefully carried up the hazardous trek. Things were going swimmingly well until their commanding officer decided there was too much talking and not enough drinking. From that point on, he decreed, it was to be ten minutes drinking time, followed by ten minutes talking. The unfortunate Captain Tony Marsh got his timings askew and began to speak out of turn. By the time he reached mid-sentence, a right hook from Mayne had laid him out cold. Marsh soon came to, and the party continued as if the incident had never occurred. As far as the men were concerned, it was just another example of their leader's volatility when under the influence. The Squadron made it back down to base without further injury, despite being a little the worse for wear. For the most part, the men regarded this period of their adventure as a vacation. Mayne had no qualms about that and was usually to be found at the heart of any drinking party. But he showed no tolerance for drinking on duty and any hint of it resulted in the offender being RTU'd immediately. Nevertheless, for these few weeks of summer on the Sicilian coast he could not begrudge their pleasure, well aware that they would be called on soon enough to put their lives on the line once more.

Chapter Eleven

Mussolini finito!

By 1 September, the Squadron was on the move again. They had just received orders from General Dempsey to capture and hold Bagnara Calabra, a small coastal town on the southwest tip of the mainland. Once more the attack would be a small but vital part of the overall Allied plan for the invasion of Italy. This would involve the Eighth Army, under the recently knighted Montgomery, crossing the Straits of Messina and launching an attack on Reggio, 11 miles to the south of Bagnara. At the same time the US Fifth Army, led by General Mark Clark, would land at Salerno, south of Naples. Montgomery would then forge northwards through Bagnara, and meet up with the Americans. Bagnara was accessible by one small road that twisted its way up from the beach, across several bridges and on through some natural tunnels, before finally reaching the town high above the beach. The Squadron would have to take the road and bridges intact and then protect the route for the oncoming Eighth Army.

This time the Americans provided the transport in the form of two LCIs (Landing Craft Infantry). They were 169 feet long, capable of holding 200 men, and were each carrying an adequate number of LCAs. The Squadron's strength was now down to 243 men of all ranks, 7 men having been RTU for leaving their posts back at Augusta. After running into mechanical trouble they were forced to carry out repairs at Riposto, before finally reaching their target at 1445 hrs on 4 September. They were now over two hours behind schedule and dawn was fast approaching.

However, their landing was completely unopposed and they quickly occupied the beach and road, neither of which had been mined. No. 3 Troop was tasked with taking and holding the road and railway to the south of the town, while 1 Troop would move through the streets and seal off the northern approaches. No. 2 Troop remained near the beach for the time being, along with the mortar detachment. Mayne then sent 1 Troop's A Section into town to test the waters. No sooner had Chris and the others entered the town than they spotted a company of German soldiers marching round a bend on the main road, about forty yards away. They opened up on the Germans, who were taken completely by surprise, wounding five and capturing twenty-eight. They also captured three MG 42 machine guns. The MG 42, or Spandau as it was known among the Allies, was a devastating weapon and the men were glad to have liberated these few from the Hun.

In the meantime, Mayne had moved Sections B and C of 1 Troop into the town, but by now the element of surprise was long gone. From high ground to the east the enemy released an onslaught of machine gun and mortar fire, killing two of the SRS and seriously wounding another seven. Despite the attack, C Section managed to find sufficient cover to hold the position, while also providing covering fire as B Section moved further to the southeast. No. 2 Troop now entered the town from the south. They moved along the main road as far as the bridge, which the Germans had already demolished. At this point they also came under fire. In the resulting skirmish, two Germans were killed. A Section now took up position at the bridgehead, while the rest of the troop probed further uphill, encountering stiff opposition as they advanced. No. 3 Troop then moved through the town and took up a covering position on its southern edge. They also attracted machine gun and mortar fire from nearby enemy troops. Returning in kind, they managed to push the Germans back, forcing them to take cover in a tunnel. Unable to use their mortar guns in the close confines, the Germans came off second best once more. Ten of their number were killed and many more wounded.

It was now approaching midday and the SRS had gained control of Bagnara, thus achieving their objective. Taking stock, Major Mayne established HQ in the town, with the mortar detachment deployed nearby. The various sections consolidated their positions and prepared for the inevitable counter-attack. Captain Gunn, who had replaced Malcolm Pleydell as the Squadron's medical orderly, busied himself with the wounded. Here, unlike their counterparts in Sicily, the civilians refused to be cowed by the fighting. They greeted the 'Inglesi' with welcoming smiles and encouraged them with cries of, 'Mussolini finito!' It was obvious to all concerned that the Germans had overstayed their welcome and that all these people wanted was to get on with their lives. The expected fightback had still not occurred by nightfall, when Mayne eventually made radio contact with the advance elements of the 15th Infantry Brigade. The Squadron seized the initiative at dawn by launching a massive mortar attack on the enemy positions. They also encountered an Italian patrol making its way towards the town from the southeast. In the resulting gunbattle the Italians scattered, but not before two were dead and several captured. By late morning the infantry began to arrive and the 15th Brigade took control of the town.

After two days of fierce fighting, the Squadron withdrew to the nearby town of Gallico, where they were billeted for a period of rest and recuperation. In the excitement of the recent fighting they had missed the news that Mussolini had been toppled from power on 4 September, and the Italian government had since signed an armistice with the Allies. While it was a cause for celebration, the men knew only too well that there were still plenty of Germans in Italy who were hell bent on holding on to it. The soldiers they had just fought in Bagnara were from the Grenadier and Jaeger regiments, and had seen action on the eastern front and in Africa. There was no reason to expect the enemy to be any less capable wherever the Squadron were next to see action. For now, Montgomery's Eighth Army was able to continue its march up the toe of Italy, and General Dempsey was most pleased with the Squadron. They had accounted for forty-seven Germans killed or wounded and had taken thirty-five prisoners. Five SRS men had been killed in action: Signalman C. Richards, Signalman W. Howell, Signalman R. Parris and Private C. Tobin all died on 4 September, while Private Ball died from his wounds the next day. Seventeen men had been wounded. Squadron doctor Captain Phil Gunn was later awarded the Military Cross for his bravery in recovering many of the wounded, while Lance Sergeant McNinch, Lance Corporal McDiarmid, and Privates Higham and Tunstall each received the Military Medal. From Gallico, the Squadron moved on to Scalea, where they relaxed while awaiting further orders. Once again, their Commander was to the fore in finding any excuse for a few drinks and a singsong. The following extract from Mortimer's *Stirling's Men*, which begins with a quote from the young officer, Peter Davis, sets the scene perfectly:

'Scarcely a night passed without him engineering a celebration of some sort,' remembered Davis. The parties followed a similar pattern; drinks all round, then Sergeant Major Rose's rich baritone and a couple of Irish tenors led by Chris O'Dowd. As the booze took effect, McNinch would be called upon to recite one of his comical monologues. Then Bob Bennett, one of the Originals of L Detachment, would croon a couple of romantic numbers. Some of the men became maudlin. Davis remembered McNinch raising a glass to Tobin. 'It's strange how always the best seem to catch it,' mumbled the Scot. 'Charlie Tobin was the best-hearted man in the section ... and here am I, a drunken old reprobate.' All the while, recounted Davis, 'Paddy would lean back, glass in hand, like some Roman emperor watching his gladiators prove their worth in the arena. At frequent stages in the evening Paddy himself would sing, usually some traditional Irish song, either sentimental or aggressive, depending on his mood at the time.' At other times he would select men to sing. 'You'd start to sing,' says (Sergeant Alfred) Youngman, 'and he would say, 'Not that, an Irish song.' 'Well, few of us knew any Irish songs.'

It was around this time also, that Chris would have been given the good news that he had been awarded the Military Medal. It was awarded in recognition of his service in North Africa, and during the Benghazi raid in particular. While his commander would have informed him that he was being recommended for the award before they left Kabrit, it was now official. On 22 September, the SRS sailed out from Scalea on board their LCI. By now their overall strength was down to 207 men. They spent the next week cruising the Mediterranean and putting in at various ports along the way. They sampled the local wines of Taranto, Brindisi and Bari, before finally berthing at Manfredonia, a small port on the Adriatic coast. Here, they were confined to the craft on one hour's sailing notice, while their commander discussed plans with General Dempsey on the quayside. When Mayne boarded the LCI to issue the new orders, he was aware that his men were about to embark on their most ambitious assault landing to date.

At noon on 2 October, they sailed out from Manfredonia on the 80-mile journey north to their target. For the first time since the Benghazi raid, they would be part of a combined operation. With them were another two LCIs containing the No. 3 Army Commando and No. 40 Marine Commando. They were bound for the port of Termoli, which lay at the eastern end of a major road that crossed the country from coast to coast. Control of this road, which ran to Campobasso on the west coast, would be vital for the Fifth Army's planned advance on Naples. The Allies also realized that the Biferno River, which reaches the sea south of Termoli, would make an ideal defensive position for the retreating Germans. General Dempsey hoped to outflank them by landing to the north of the river.

The plan was for No. 3 Commando to lead the assault and establish a beachhead. The SRS and No. 40 Commando would then follow ashore, the Commando to take the harbour while the SRS would move inland and take control of the roads and bridges. Mayne had been advised that the Germans were holding the high ground that overlooked the river. He planned to attack their rear and create havoc among the enemy's defensive positions. As they approached Termoli in the early hours of 3 October, the night was dead still and practically moonless. Many of the men had an uneasy sense of foreboding, mindful, no doubt of the cock-up at Benghazi. Waiting on deck, Bob McDougall noticed the darkening mood of his friend, Lance Corporal John 'Ginger' Hodgkinson. 'What's the matter?' he enquired. 'I've got a sneaking feeling I won't be coming back from this one,' Hodgkinson replied. At 0245 hrs, the SRS was given the signal to land from the men of 3 Commando, who had already taken up position on the beach. After coming ashore the Squadron quickly organized into its various sections and forged inland towards their particular targets.

The Germans were waiting for them, but had expected the attack to come from the southeast, not the west. As a result, those who were dug in facing the southeast began to withdraw, in order to adjust their defensive positioning. Officer John Tonkin, leading B Section of 3 Troop, came upon some stragglers as they came to a bridge on the Campomarino road just before dawn. They shot up the German truck, killing one man and capturing the three survivors. The section moved further inland, coming under frequent fire, and at first light found themselves at the foot of a small valley. They quickly realized they were surrounded by scores of Germans, who suddenly opened fire from the hills that flanked the valley. Reluctantly, Tonkin gave the order: 'Every man for himself.' Lance

Corporal Joe Fassam became the first casualty of the raid when he attempted to break out, while the rest of the section, apart from six men who hid out, were taken prisoner. Within minutes, A Section 3 Troop entered the valley and this time their enemy had lost the element of surprise. In the firefight that followed Staff Sergeant Nobby Clarke and Captain Bob Melot were wounded. Both men insisted on carrying on after receiving First Aid. Clarke continued leading his men while Melot, the oldest member of the Squadron at fifty-four, returned to the fray with his arm in a sling. After the last shot was fired, five Germans lay dead and nine had been captured.

After briefly interrogating the German prisoners and examining their insignia, the men quickly realized the high calibre of the enemy in their clutches. Their prisoners belonged to the 16th Panzer Division, who had just arrived from fighting the Fifth Army at the Salerno landings. The unit had a fearsome reputation and had recently been replenished, after suffering huge losses at Stalingrad the previous winter. They had hiked over 90 miles of mountainous terrain to defend Termoli, and they were not alone. Allied intelligence sources had already indicated the presence of an estimated 600 Germans in the town. Many were ordinary garrison soldiers, but among them was a platoon of the 1st Parachute Division. This was an elite unit who had become extremely battle hardened, having seen action all over Europe. It was during the invasion of Crete however that they really made their mark. The men of 2 Troop did not have long to wait before they also had a chance to test their mettle with Hitler's best. As they advanced towards their targets they came under heavy machine gun fire from some nearby farmhouses. The Squadron's mortar section immediately set to work, and the combined effect of mortar and Bren gun soon had the desired effect. Nine Germans were captured during the mop up.

At 0530 hrs, No. 1 Troop had also reached the road to Campomarino. Unlike the other two troops, they had not split into sections. Their target was a bridge at the western edge of the town. With daylight approaching they had taken to wading waist high along the road's ditches. Suddenly, they heard German voices coming from a nearby farmhouse. The Germans had obviously been alerted by the sound of gunfire from the town, and were frantically rushing about and revving an engine. In their eagerness to support their chums however, they had failed to notice the water-sodden cluster of desperados crouching in the ditches around them. Over forty years later, Reg Seekings relived the encounter:

We poured out of the ditches, where they were defending the road. There was a three-wheeled track motorcycle pulling a recoilless gun – one of the first we saw – and we realized then this was Airborne, because they were the only troops that had them then. There were twenty-odd piled onto this bike and trailer, all laughing and chatting. So we ran – got over the ditch we were wading through, to keep under cover a bit, stop ourselves from being skylined. I've never experienced fire like it. Those lads of mine were bloody magnificent. They opened up and the air was thick with lead. Practically cut chunks of it out. And in seconds, they'd gone. It pinned the driver, he was killed immediately, and all of 'em, in seconds ... Then the action started. And then we found out that it was the German 1st Parachute Division, the people from Crete – they had Cretan armbands – and we had all morning fighting them. It was one of their company command posts at this farmhouse. We had quite a battle there with them until Alec Muirhead, a mortar man managed to make contact with them. He could see me, and so I said: 'Can you see me?' He said: 'Yes.' I said: 'Well, aim on me plus twenty-five, and you'll be spot on.' I had that confidence in this man. He was fantastic with the mortar. So he aimed on me plus twenty-five and we wiped 'em out.

These people were either dead or wounded before they surrendered. Their major was a huge chap. Everyone was wounded, even he had got wounds. When they came in, one, a lieutenant, was being carried on a stretcher, and that was his young brother, and this major said: 'Please shoot him he's beyond it.' And he was; his stomach was all blown out. So Chalky White finished him off, and this major just blinked and he said: 'The trouble is with you people, you are too hard.' I said: 'Well that's good, coming from people like you.' They'd been in Crete and all over; they were prouder of their Cretan armbands than of their Iron Crosses. But when he saw us he said: 'Ah! SAS – I said to my men, "This is strange, I've never known men to fight this hard." If I had known we would never have fought like this.' I said: 'Why not?' He said: 'What? Good men kill good men? Our job is to kill the ordinary troops. You

131

kill the panzer people, the tank people, the infantry. But you don't kill each other.' That was their attitude. I can't understand it; it was amazing.

Shortly after, the troop pulled out and eventually reached the bridge, only to learn from the locals that the Germans had destroyed it the previous day. While they sat about brewing-up, they spotted some infantry men, part of 11 Brigade, trekking up a nearby ridge and taking up position there. Their demeanour appeared to be very casual in Seekings' eyes and he immediately sought out their colonel to warn him of the danger: 'I got a blast from him,' he admits, 'told to mind my own bloody business; I was just a bloody sergeant and he'd take no advice from a sergeant. A few seconds later he'd lost the biggest part of his men, hundreds of them. Oh God, you've never seen casualties like it in your life. They wouldn't believe me that they were walking right into the 88 area, where all the batteries were. They were really slaughtered, mown down by all sorts of fire.'

At midday, Mayne reviewed progress. The men of Squadron HQ had already seen action earlier in the day, when they had confronted a party of Germans and taken most of them prisoner. They had now positioned themselves at a crossroads to the southeast, in close proximity to No. 1 Troop. Going on the continual flow of information from the radio reports from his sections, he was in a reasonable position to gauge both the calibre and morale of the enemy. They were many of them, and they were very capable fighters. By now, Mayne was well aware of the presence of the 1st Parachute Division in the town. Despite this, the response to the landings had been somewhat fragmented, and there was a discernable aura of apathy among many of the prisoners. That some of them felt disheartened was understandable, given that they were now defending a country that had turned its back on them and switched sides. As a result, gathering information on ammunition dumps and deployments was a relatively easy task.

The afternoon passed without further incident, and a formidable defensive position was now in place, with the SRS on the left flank, 40 Commando to the right and 3 Commando holding the centre. The 2nd Lancashire Fusiliers, as part of the 11 Brigade, eventually arrived to relieve the Squadron. Once again, Mayne could reflect on a job well done: the SRS had achieved its objectives by means of guile and efficiency. Lance Corporal Fassam had been the only fatality, and had been buried by the roadside near the Squadron HQ. Three men had been wounded while twenty-three were missing, presumed captured. On the other hand, twenty-three Germans had died in the fighting, seventeen were wounded and thirty-nine captured. The Squadron was now ordered back to Termoli, where they were to be billeted in the local monastery. As the men wound down at their new quarters, they were all too mindful that it was likely to be a very brief respite. They began sorting out and replacing their weapons and equipment, the talk being all about the possibility of a counter-attack. The Germans were unlikely to take the loss of Termoli lying down for very long, and the loss of the natural defensive line of the Biferno River was a setback their High Command could not afford. The only question was where and when they would mount their counter-attack.

The night of 3 October saw the day's light drizzle turn to incessant heavy rain. Back at their billets, Chris and his mates forgot about the fighting and enjoyed a well-earned rest. There was no sign of any enemy contact, and the men relaxed in the usual way; chatting up the local girls, drinking bottles of the local wine and singing to their hearts' content. Outside, the worsening weather conditions impeded the Allies' progress. The pontoon bridges they had assembled to replace the blown ones were in constant danger of being swept away in the flood. In contrast, the enemy build-up was proceeding unhindered. By now the entire 16th Panzer Division had made the journey from Salerno and, as they regrouped outside the town, they got the order to recapture Termoli at any cost.

Chapter Twelve

Tragedy at Termoli

'It's shattering, because these were the first men I'd actually commanded. When I say "commanded", I had always been working with John or Stirling in small parties, and I'd never had any men really of my own. And this time I'd had men which I'd trained, new men, and moulded them together. And so you had a real rapport with them, and they were good, they were more than ... And it'd been a long campaign too, and they'd become more than just your men; they were your friends, your pals.'

Reg Seekings

By dawn the next morning there were several British regiments in Termoli. The 2nd Battalion Lancashire Fusiliers, the 5th Battalion East Kents, the 6th Battalion Royal West Kents, the 56th Reconnaissance Regiment, the 8th Battalion Argyll and Sutherland Highlanders, had all arrived in the town and were already advancing. It was beginning to look like the SRS would be surplus to requirements after all. The monastery, which overlooked the harbour, was draughty and damp and Mayne and his fellow officers had already moved across the street. The house he chose was fitted out with deep shag pile carpets and the best of furniture, including a billiard table and a gramophone.

Shortly after 1230 hrs on 4 October, however, he had an urgent message from HQ: a large build-up of German troops had been spotted near the railway station to the west of Termoli, and the 11 Brigade were thin on the ground and under pressure. In fact, neither Mayne nor his men across the road were aware of the worsening situation on the outskirts of the town. Almost from first light, when the Germans had moved some tanks tentatively towards the defensive lines, the British units had been slowly pulling back. Mayne was ordered to supply one troop from the Squadron to relieve the situation. Sections A and C of No. 2 Troop, along with C Section of No. 1 Troop, under the command of Captains Tony Marsh and Derrick Harrison, were eventually picked for the job. They boarded two 3-ton trucks and headed off along the narrow road towards the station. By the time they got there, however, the attack had petered out. The men spent an uneventful night at their new position, where the main problem was the freezing conditions. That night also, a German Artillery observer, complete with radio, infiltrated the town and set up an ideal observation post in a local church tower. There, he bedded down for the night and waited for morning.

Having enjoyed a quiet night at the monastery, Chris and his friends had a rude awakening on the morning of 5 October. The sound of shellfire and heavy machine-guns soon reverberated all over the town, as the Germans made their intentions clear. About a dozen German bombers then swooped over the harbour in a vicious attack. Both the 6th Royal West Kents and the 5th Battalion East Kents had already abandoned their positions and were retreating towards the main Termoli to Larino road. The main thrust of the attack now came from the high ground further inland, where the Argyll and Sutherland Highlanders were positioned. Here the 64th Panzer Grenadier Regiment and a battalion of the 79th Panzer Grenadiers pushed the Scots back to the local brickworks. By midday, they had abandoned the building. By 1400 hrs, a furious Brigadier Howlett had met with the officers in charge of the various regiments. He forbade any more withdrawals and ordered that the new positions were to be held to the last man.

Meanwhile, the SRS men holed up near the station were coming under persistent heavy shelling from anti-aircraft guns which had been adapted for a ground role, as well as the usual mortar and heavy machine-gun fire. Captain Harry Poat, 2 Troop Commander, then radioed through with fresh orders: C Section of 2 Troop was to enter a wooded area where the 56th Reconnaissance Regiment had been taking a pounding from the tanks of the 16th Panzers. The section came upon a scene of carnage, with dead and wounded men lying among their destroyed equipment. They could see immediately that there was no hope of holding their position, and eventually returned safely to their comrades, who were still holding firm.

Captain Marsh now ordered his men to probe further northwards. The enemy reacted immediately by directing a hail of fire in their direction. A mortar explosion then injured four men. Lance Corporal Sid Payne did his best to administer First Aid, but with no morphine at hand there was little he could do apart from some basic bandaging. Ginger Hodgkinson's injury appeared to be the most serious. He was in intense pain from a shrapnel wound which had shattered his back, and to Payne it looked like Ginger's war might be over. 'He was in agony,' according to Payne. 'The normal field dressing we carried was no use for him and he kept asking me to shoot him.'

The section was in a hopeless position by now and Marsh made the wise decision to withdraw immediately. Carrying Hodgkinson on an old barn door, the men edged their way towards a culvert, hoping to find cover. After a brief respite the German marksmen found their range once more, pinning down the SRS men and making any movement impossible. Following a head count, it was discovered that several men were now missing – presumably lost during the flight to the culvert. The situation was getting worse. Ginger Hodgkinson died from his wounds, before his mates had a chance to get him proper medical care. At dusk, the rest of the men were finally able to make their way towards the town via the beach, where they met up with Captain Poat and some others. He detailed three men, Bob McDougall, Ginger Hines and James McDiarmid, with the task of carrying the wounded back to the aid post and through the town.

This was a mission fraught with danger, particularly from the likelihood of sniper attack. Progress was slow along the darkening narrow streets, as the stretcher-bearers nervously picked their way. 'I'd stopped for a fag,' recalled McDougall, 'when this Italian looked out of a window with a rifle and pointed it at the other two. He hadn't seen me so I gave him a burst. He ducked down and McDiarmid went in after him. When he came out he said, "He'll fire that Beretta no more. I wrapped it round his fucking head."' The German counter-attack had emboldened the few Italians with Fascist leanings that remained in the town, and the SRS party had just bumped into one. They eventually managed to hand their mates over to the medics before making it safely back to the monastery. Sadly, another one of the wounded, Private B. McLaughlan would die later from his injuries on 12 October.

The situation was deteriorating by the hour as the German thrust continued unchecked. Earlier in the day, acting Staff Captain Leese had been killed outright when a shell hit the Brigade HQ. At approximately 1430 hrs, Paddy Mayne was enjoying a game of billiards with fellow officers Bill Fraser, Pat Reilly and Phil Gunn the medical orderly, when the order came through: every available man was required to take up a defensive position along the Termoli–Larino road to prevent the Germans breaking through. Across the road, Reg Seekings had been relaxing in a café when he got wind that something was up: 'The brigadier was in there with some of his officers, and a despatch rider came in with a dispatch. I heard the brigadier say: "We'd better get the SRS on this,"' Mayne's reaction to the order stunned the others in the room. 'He just carried on with the game,' Reilly remembered. 'I thought to myself, well if you can do it, chum, I'll do it with you. And we did. We finished the game and then went out to get things sorted.' Meanwhile, Seekings had gone back to the monastery to warn his men to be at the ready. Chris and his mates had been listening to the sounds of battle all day, now they were about to be part of it. By this time, Captain Marsh and his men were being pinned down back at the culvert. Mayne ordered every available man, including the cooks and clerks, to head for a nearby cemetery where the thrust of the assault seemed to be concentrated.

Five captured German trucks were lined up outside the monastery to take the men to the fighting. As they came out on the street, a family of locals gathered to see them off. They had been providing a laundry service for the men since their arrival, and had been very friendly. Chris and his section were ordered to board the first truck by Seekings. Standing nearby were No. 1 Troop Commander Bill Fraser, and Johnny Wiseman. Driving the truck was Sergeant Bill McNinch, who had volunteered for the job despite being injured. As McNinch pulled up beside the men, however, Seekings found the truck already full with the remaining section of 2 Troop. Wiseman immediately ordered them out of the back and his own boys piled in. The confusion left Seekings feeling uneasy: 'We were browned off. Next minute we'd get blown to hell, because we knew Jerry had the range. After messing around the first salvoes started to come over, and I was all: "Come on let's get moving." We'd just had the order to get off, and I was just kicking the fastening loose on the

138

back of the tailboard, and the next thing, Christ, a God Almighty crash and explosion, and one landed right smack in the truck.'

The whole street shuddered under the impact as the 105 mm shell hit the truck. Pat Reilly had been lifted and thrown by the explosion like a rag doll: 'The next thing I knew I was halfway down the street,' he recalled, 'lying on my back, laughing like hell. It must have been shock.' Pieces of molten rubber and metal, mixed with flesh and blood, splattered the buildings and trees nearby. The acrid smoke hanging overhead began to slowly clear, and a sickly smell that was a mixture of cordite, blood and burning flesh lingered in the air. Each man had been carrying up to twelve 2lb anti-tank grenades around their waists, which had detonated on impact and worsened the carnage. The Italian family who had been waiting to wave them off paid dearly for their friendly gesture. The parents had been killed, and their young son of about twelve was running around screaming with his guts hanging out. Reg Seekings, who had miraculously escaped uninjured, did the kindest thing, under the circumstances: 'I had to shoot him. There was absolutely no hope for him, and you couldn't let anybody suffer like that. So I caught him and shot him – there was nothing you could do.' A body lay burning on the ground beside him. When Seekings returned with water to put it out, he recognized the charred body as being that of Alex Skinner, a young lad from Essex who had also recently been awarded the Military Medal. Sitting in the cab of the lorry, which remained more or less intact, Bill McNinch was apparently still in one piece. As Seekings attempted to rouse him however, he realized he had been cut in two by a piece of shrapnel.

Johnny Wiseman was another to escape unscathed, although the man he had been talking with was hurled some 60 yards through a second-floor window. Only his torso was ever found. Bob Lowson was inside having his wounds dressed when he was asked to help. What he came upon was, 'a mess, absolutely terrible . . . Spike Kerr was lying on the ground praying to God to help him. Lunt, the padre, came up and slapped him across the face: "You are not going to die," he told him.' Bill Fraser was just sitting there with a blank expression on his face, and blood spurting from a shrapnel wound in the shoulder. Beside him stood Graham Gilmour, with one of his eyeballs hanging from its socket. Seekings then came upon the body of Titch Davison, the young lad who had told General Dempsey to 'stuff it'. He was barely sixteen years old. He was still recognizable, although his face was badly damaged. As the section leader attempted to move him, however, his shattered body just fell apart. Pete Davis, commander of 2 Troop, saw that one of the Italian girls was still alive, and was now sitting pitifully beside the mutilated bodies of her parents. Glancing upwards, he realized the lump of flesh hanging on a wire was a human scalp. He immediately recognized the distinctive curly black locks as belonging to Chris. He spun away and vomited by the side of the road.

By now Phil Gunn, the medical officer, was on the scene. He concentrated his attention on those who had a chance of pulling through. Johnny Wiseman was walking among the carnage half dazed, trying to calculate how many men he had lost from his section. It did not look encouraging: 'I'd been with those chaps for three months,' he remembered. 'And with one shell I'd lost them. But what could I do? It was the luck of the draw, it was war. You just accepted it.' In fact only Seekings, Gilmour and one other were still standing. The other man never spoke again, according to Seekings. Several days later he was found banging his head on a brick wall and was promptly RTU'd. Although it was never spoken about, it is thought that two of the men were so seriously injured that they were put out of their misery on the spot. The German artillery observer, still holed up in the church tower, must have been pleased with his day's work: eighteen men had been killed or mortally wounded. In one foul swoop he had dealt the SAS the highest mortality strike it had ever suffered in a single incident. His luck would run out only hours later however, when some members of No. 3 Marine Commando surrounded him at the church. As they climbed the tower they ordered him to surrender. Responding with a pistol shot, he was finally shot down by a burst of Bren gun fire as he tried to escape across the rooftops.

Reg Seekings had no doubt as to where the blame lay for the massacre:

I don't know why the delay occurred. This is the typical sort of thing that you get. It's the old story very often – you're highly trained, specialised training, and you come under the command of a man that hasn't done one iota of specialised training. But the mere fact that he's an officer, and particularly a senior officer – he knows a damned sight more than you do, and he's allowed to direct you. And this is where the whole thing breaks

140

down. This brigadier, he was hopeless. Shocking. Indecision, no decisions. All that on/off was all him, nothing to do with Paddy. Brigade kept sending messages. I knew where Paddy was, so I thought: Well the best thing I can do is go and report this all to Paddy, and they said they would bury the mess.

As it turned out, Johnny Wiseman was the first to break the news to their commander. Mayne made no direct comment but his eyes had a deathly stare. He then told Wiseman to attach the survivors to his own HQ Troop and make for the cemetery right away, as the Germans were about to break through.

When Mayne himself got to the cemetery, his Squadron was taking a pounding from the enemy anti-tank guns. The Marine Commandos were taking the brunt of the attack, with Mayne and most of the SRS to their left. On the right near the railway line were the 40 Commando and the remainder of the SRS under Harry Poat. All around them the British infantrymen were abandoning their positions and running off in panic. Harry Poat could no longer disguise his disgust: meeting up with an officer of the 78th Division, he pointed to the man's shoulder flash and enquired what the insignia was. The officer answered that it was a battleaxe. 'It should be a knitting needle,' was Poat's caustic reply. At 1715 hrs three German tanks attacked along the railway line. With only one 6-pound anti-tank gun and some accurate Bren gun fire, the defenders stood firm and managed to stem the onslaught.

At first light on the morning of 6 October, a couple of German fighters swooped over the men but were quickly chased off by a squadron of Spitfires. Then came some unexpected good news, for a change: the 38th Irish Brigade had landed on the beach during the night, and were now preparing for a major assault. The news perked Mayne up immediately and he was heard to say, 'You'll be all right now lads, the Irish are coming and they'll sort it all out for us.' True to the word of the SRS commander, the 6th Inniskilling Fusiliers and 1st Royal Irish Fusiliers soon advanced and began to dominate the battle. A dozen Canadian tanks led the way, making the Fusiliers' famous Gaelic motto, *Fág An Beallach* (Clear the Way), even more appropriate. In the evening the brigade's third battalion, the 2nd London Irish Rifles, who had held back while the Fusiliers advanced, mopped up any resistance they came across, and the battle for Termoli was finally over.

Slowly the men made their way back to the monastery. They arrived back in dribs and drabs, many too exhausted or disgusted to talk about the previous thirty-six hours. The SRS had suffered more than any other British regiment in the defence of Termoli: twenty-one men had been killed, twenty-four wounded and twenty-three missing. In comparison, 3 Commando lost five men and 40 Commando, six. Nevertheless, the Germans had been beaten and it was time to bury the dead. Sid Payne had the misfortune to be picked as one of the five-man burial detail who had to collect the remains: 'I knew Chris O'Dowd was dead because his scalp was strung across the telephone wires and we had to get a pole to poke it down,' he remembers. Padre Lunt wrapped the remains in blankets, as the graves were dug in the south corner of a convent garden near the seafront. As the Squadron gathered at the gravesides to bury their fallen comrades, Alex Muirhead remembered the poem he had found in the pocket of a dead German:

I wonder God if you'll check my hand
Somehow I feel you will understand
Funny I have come to this hellish place
Before I had time to see your face
Well, I guess there isn't much more to say
But I'm sure glad God I met you today.

The Squadron spent a further six days in Termoli; it was not a happy time. It was a bitter blow for a small closely-knit outfit like the SRS, to have lost so many pals all at once. The persistent winter rain seemed to match the moroseness of the men, and getting drunk did little to lift the mood. Terry Moore explained: 'When you took the first drink it was in relief that you had survived, the second was that you would be able to take part in the next action and the third would be for your fallen comrades who had not been so lucky.' It was at this point also, that another of the famous 'Mayne myths' was born. Several accounts would have us believe that Mayne went on his own private man-hunt, stopping only when he believed he had exacted suitable revenge on the Germans. These versions of what happened may have the ring of truth about them, but are most likely exaggerated. On 10 October they had another visit from General Dempsey who paid them the following tribute:

It is just three months since we landed in Sicily and during that time you have carried out four successful operations. You were originally only lent to me for the first operation, that of Capo Murro di Porco. That was a brilliant operation, brilliantly planned and brilliantly carried out. Your orders were to capture and destroy a coastal battery, but you did more. I left it entirely up to you what you did after that and you went on to capture two more batteries and a very large number of prisoners, an excellent piece of work. No one then could have foretold that things would have turned out as they have. You were to have returned to the Middle East after that operation but you then went on to take Augusta. You had no time for careful planning, but still you were highly successful. Then came Bagnara and finally Termoli. The landing at Termoli completely upset the Germans' schedule and the balance of their forces by introducing a threat to the north of Rome. They were obliged to bring to the east coast the 16th Panzer Division that was in reserve in the Naples area. They had orders, which have since come into our hands, to recapture Termoli at all costs and drive the British into the sea. These orders, thanks to you, they were unable to carry out. It had another effect though, it eased the pressure on the American Fifth Army and as you have probably heard, they are now advancing. When I first saw you at Az Zib and told you that you were going to work with 13 Corps, I was very impressed by you and all that I saw. When I told you that you had a coastal battery to destroy, I was convinced that it was the right sort of job for you. In all my Military career, and in my time I have commanded many units, but I have never met a unit in which I had such confidence as I have in yours, and I mean that.

The very next day General Montgomery showed up, but the contrast could not have been more pronounced. The men were simply not in the mood for self-promoting speeches. He made some vague promise about always having the SRS by his side, but no one was holding their breath – he had apparently given much the same speech to a unit of Canadians some time earlier. On 12 October, the Squadron embarked for Molfetta, 175 miles further down the Adriatic coast. Here, they remained for the rest of the month recuperating and resting, before finally sailing back to Britain. Termoli was to be the last and most costly operation in the Squadron's Mediterranean campaign.

Chapter Thirteen

Aftermath

On 23 October, Chris's parents James and Sarah received a letter from the Irish Guards, congratulating them on their son's award of the Military Medal. They would have opened the letter with some trepidation, preparing themselves for the worst possible news – but that was still to come. 'In case you have not seen the papers,' the letter ran, 'it is with great pleasure I have to inform you that your son no. 2719054 L/Sgt. Christopher O'Dowd, has been awarded the Military Medal in the London Gazette of the 12th October, 1943.' Four weeks later, came the news they had dreaded. The letter was written by Major R.C. Alexander of the Irish Guards, on 19 November – over six weeks after Chris was killed. Word would soon have travelled around the village and local people would have felt truly sorry for the death of such a popular young lad. The women, in particular would have felt a great sympathy for Sarah, having lost the youngest of her surviving sons. But their pity would have been accompanied by the contention that it had all been for nothing. After all, Chris owed no loyalty to Britain and had no need to go fighting her wars. The best anyone could say was that it was a tragic waste of a young life.

Without a body to mourn, the only alternative left to the family was to have Mass celebrated for the repose of Chris's soul at the local church in Shrule. Meanwhile, the SRS were experiencing some difficulty finding Chris's home address. This was understandable, given the Squadron's nomadic nature, and the first to do so was Lieutenant G.N. Disinan, who eventually wrote to Sarah in late November. Sarah's reply was dated the 8th of December, and the depth of her grief is all too apparent in the words she wrote:

Dear Sir,
I have picked up courage at last to write to you to thank you for writing and letting me know about my son's death. I know you

found it hard to write but it was much better to let me know the worst had happened. I must say I was terribly shocked and grieved and so was my husband and family when the sad news reached here. If that news came a few months earlier or even a few weeks, it would not be quite such a shock, as I was often expecting to hear of his death. But I was just after receiving news of him being awarded the Military Medal in the London Gazette and it gave me such hopes of seeing him again. Now I know I will never again see Christopher in this world. It is so very sad but I must only say, God's Holy Will be done.

I'm very glad that my son Christopher was so brave and that he didn't mind giving his life in self-sacrifice. He must have faced death bravely, even that is a comfort to know. Yet there are many other things I would like to know about him. Perhaps you would get a chance to write to me some other day and if there is any little thing that you know, I would be so glad to hear again from you. Was Christy able to keep in touch with a Chaplain? If you are a Catholic, you will understand how anxious every mother is about her son's spiritual welfare. I only hope God has spared you and will continue to watch over you to the end, and give you strength to fight the enemy. You were kind to write to me. I often think if there is any mark over Christy's lonely grave or will there ever be a chance of getting a snap of it. I understand that he was buried in Italy.

I was also wondering if his personal belongings were saved – there may be some medals or letters that I could have. I want you to know that I'm not holding you responsible for anything. I'm just asking you as Christy's friend, and I trust you will forgive a lonely mother, as I still think I should hear from him. I can hardly believe he is dead, R.I.P.

I will now finish, again thanking you for your letter and your kind words about my son, Christopher. You will always be remembered in our family prayers.

The letter was promptly passed on to Paddy Mayne, who was anxious to offer his sympathy. Mayne made a point of writing personally to the next of kin of all the men who died under his command, and Sarah's letter was found among his papers many years later. A tantalizing snippet of his reply was drafted in pencil beside it: 'I have been feeling for a long time that I would very much like to write to you but until lately I have been unable to get your address. I would like to offer you and your husband and family my sincere sympathy on the death of your son, Christopher. I knew him well, and on many raids ...' Unfortunately, that is all that remains of the correspondence between Sarah and the SAS Commander. On 30 March, Chris's possessions, such as they were, were sent back to his parents. The army form list tells its own story: Chris's worldly possessions amounted to two wristwatches, rosary beads and some letters – a soldier of fortune, he certainly wasn't. Nevertheless, knowing he had kept rosary beads brought some comfort to his heartbroken mother.

The next letter to arrive at Cahernabruck from the Army was an invitation to James and Sarah to attend 'a ceremony for presentation by His Majesty the King of the Military Medal awarded to your late son, as soon as the ban on civilian travel to and from this country is lifted.' It came from the War Office and was dated 15 May 1944. More letters were sent back and forth before it was finally decided that Chris's brother Martin would receive the medal. The travel ban was in force but fortunately Martin was still living in Heston. It must have been a proud day for him on 20 February 1945, when King George handed him his brother's award at Buckingham Palace. In the meantime, arrangements were being made to re-inter the remains of Chris and his comrades in a proper War Cemetery. On 26 October 1944, the War Office wrote to James and Sarah again, this time to inform them that Chris was now buried in the Sangro River Cemetery, Italy. It was another small consolation to know he now had a proper grave, although in truth the convent wasn't such a bad choice in the circumstances.

Although Sarah never got to see Chris's grave, many of his siblings and their children have made the journey down through the years. Around the village of Shrule life went on, and Chris soon became yesterday's news. The fledgling state known as Eire or the Irish Free State was still in the process of finding a new identity in the world, and young men who died fighting for the 'old enemy' were not a cause for celebration. De Valera's neutrality position was still holding firm and the only time he had deviated from it publicly, was when he voiced his disapproval at Germany's invasion of the Low Countries in 1940. Essentially, he saw neutrality as the best way of preserving the nation's sovereignty. His position continued to infuriate Churchill, who had failed in his efforts to lease back some strategic Irish ports for the duration of the war. The situation between the two leaders eventually descended into a sometimes undignified public slanging match carried out over the airwaves. The people backed De Valera's stance on the neutrality issue, but despite all Churchill's bluster, they were in the words of a popular saying of the time; 'being neutral against Germany.'

Over 1,500 Allied aircraft, mostly sea-planes, took advantage of Foynes airport on the west coast, and Allied planes were allowed to over-fly County Donegal on their way to bases in Northern Ireland. Several Allied planes crash-landed in the south, and their occupants were immediately and discreetly transported across the border. At the same time there were a number of German nationals in custody, having been accused of spying. De Valera also took the precaution of locking up the majority of the IRA in internment camps, believing they would seize the occasion to destabilize the State. As a result, they were not in a position to take advantage, and apart from a botched operation to import Nazi weapons codenamed 'Plan Kathleen', they posed little threat to State security. When 900 people were killed in a single bombing raid on Belfast, the Southern Irish authorities sent fire-tenders to help. Later on, the D-Day planners depended greatly on the Irish weather reports as the time approached to launch their invasion. As the end of hostilities drew near however, De Valera managed to outrage not only Churchill, but also most of the civilized world by offering his sympathy, on behalf of the Irish people, to the German Embassy on hearing of Hitler's suicide. He was the only European leader to do so, but to his way of thinking he was merely following the correct protocol. His stubborn streak was also at work, and the last thing he wanted was to be accused of cosying up to the victors, now that the war was over.

After the war, Churchill and De Valera were both rejected by their people in following General Elections. But like his adversary, De Valera's loss of power in 1948 was only temporary and he was re-elected in 1951. People in Southern Ireland now wanted to forget about the war and looked forward to better times. Following the Great War, a memorial had been planned for Islandbridge in Dublin, and although it was now finally completed, it was largely ignored. The Free State had become a republic during De Valera's absence and had finally broken completely with what was left of the British Empire. Many of the 70,000 young men who had fought for

148

the British Army chose not to return home. Those who did were treated more or less with indifference, and on some occasions with open hostility. Remembrance Day was a British commemoration of a war their country had chosen to ignore, so it too was dismissed out of hand. There was no such thing as 'Poppy Day' and nobody wore them any more. In 1923, 150,000 poppies had been sold around the country but those days were long over. Remembrance Day gatherings, such as they were, were frequently attacked by Sinn Fein mobs who objected to both the playing of the British National Anthem and the flying of the Union Jack. Many of these returning solders were made to feel like strangers in their own country and seldom spoke of the war. Thousands of their fellow-countrymen had given their lives for the preservation of democracy, yet they remained forgotten and uncelebrated for decades. To this day, the only statue dedicated to a casualty of the Second World War in the Republic of Ireland is a bust of Sean Russell, the IRA Chief of Staff, at Fairview Park in Dublin. Russell, seen by many as an Irish 'Quisling', did not even have the distinction of dying in action. He died of a perforated ulcer on board a German submarine, while taking part in the later aborted 'Plan Kathleen' in 1940. The plan entailed landing German troops on the west coast, and invading the North from a base in County Leitrim. The statue was originally unveiled in 1951 by the IRA and Sinn Fein, with the blessing of Dublin Corporation. Republicans were just beginning to flex their muscles again, having been interned for the duration of the war, and the unveiling drew a crowd of 5,000 people. By then De Valera was back in power and his secret police kept a good eye on the proceedings. The monument has been vandalized many times over the years but it still stands to this day.

The returning soldiers were not disappointed by their lukewarm reception, they had expected as much. Their reasons for joining up had been many and varied: A small number would have owed their political allegiance to Britain, being Anglo-Irish to begin with. Many would have been conscripted in Britain, where the only alternatives were the coalmines or prison. Almost 5,000 deserted the Irish Army to defend democracy and were promptly court martialled in absentia. But the majority were lads like Chris, eager to get in on the act and see the world. He was only one of an estimated 3,000 men from south of the border who died fighting for the British Army, but Chris was no ordinary soldier. As a free spirit, he was bound naturally to thoughts of adventure, and staying in the west of

Ireland was never an option. Driven by a fierce individualistic streak, he was determined to go his own way in the world despite the advice of his family and friends.

Coupled with his want of excitement was an unshakable belief that he was on the right side. He had been politically aware since his teenage years, and was well aware of the evils of Fascism. After returning from his leave with the Irish Guards in 1940, he was not content to hang around the barracks while the top brass decided how to use them next. Browned off by the endless drills and parades, the Commandos were his way out, and he took his chance with both hands. He went on to cut the mustard with the legendary L Detachment SAS, and fought alongside the most decorated British soldier of the war, the enigmatic Blair 'Paddy' Mayne. Ironically, his old comrades in the 1st Battalion, Irish Guards, ended up in Italy shortly after his death. They went on to suffer very heavy losses at Anzio in 1944 and the Battalion never fully recovered. They had landed at the beachhead in February with a strength of 1,080 and by the time they withdrew to Naples on 7 March, they were down to twenty officers and 247 other ranks. With that kind of odds, it is unlikely Chris would have survived anyway.

But what if Paddy Mayne had cut short his billiards game, or Johnny Wiseman had not insisted on Chris's section taking the first truck? Chris knew the score as well as the next man: he had lived life to the limit for as long as he had it, and his death had not been a long drawn-out affair, but had come in an instant. The SAS men he fought with had a unique camaraderie, and depended on one another in the heat of battle, they were the original 'band of brothers'. While researching his book, *Stirling's Men*, Gavin Mortimer had the privilege of interviewing over sixty of Chris's former comrades in their later years. Not one man had a bad word to say about him, either as a soldier or as a friend.

In recent years some effort has been made to acknowledge the debt owed by the nation to the likes of young men like Chris. In 1995, the then Taoiseach, John Bruton, paid tribute to those who 'volunteered to fight against Nazi tyranny in Europe, at least 10,000 of whom were killed while serving in British uniforms ... In recalling their bravery, we are recalling a shared experience of Irish and British people ... We remember a British part of the inheritance of all who live in Ireland.' He was speaking at the recently renovated Islandbridge War Memorial. A Remembrance Day ceremony is now held annually at St Patrick's Cathedral, with the President in attendance. The Mayo Peace Park was opened on 7 October by President Mary McAleese to honour those from Mayo 'who served and died in all wars worldwide and conflicts of the past century, with the Allied and Commonwealth forces – a forgotten generation who were written out of local history until recent times.' After some initial confusion regarding his postal address, Chris's name was eventually added to the list of men honoured in stone at Castlebar. His name also appears in the Roll of Honour to Irish Second World War fatalities* on show at Trinity College, Dublin. The Roll was compiled by Dr Yvonne McEwen of the University of Edinburgh and presented to the College by her, on 12 June 2009.

---

*In total 7,507 Irish men and women died serving for the British in the Second World War. Some 3,890 came from the North, while 3,617 came from the neutral Free State. *Source*: Dr Yvonne McEwen.

Epilogue

Having returned to Britain, the Squadron was given back its original name, the SAS, and went on to play a pivotal role in the D-Day landings. They were dropped behind enemy lines and linked up with the French Resistance to create their own particular brand of havoc. When the war finally ended, the SAS was officially disbanded and the men went their separate ways. It looked like the end for the regiment, but in 1950 it was reformed. The new SAS was later sent to Malaya, with the blessing of Churchill who had recently been returned to power.

DAVID STIRLING made four escape attempts before finally being sent to Colditz, where he remained for the rest of the war. After his release he went to Rhodesia to try his hand at business. While there he founded the Capricorn Africa Society, a group dedicated to the promotion of racial harmony. He returned to Britain in the 1970s where he was involved in the security business. He died in 1990, having been knighted earlier the same year. In 2003 a statue of the great leader was unveiled at Dunblane, near his home in Scotland.

BLAIR 'PADDY' MAYNE was one of those who found it difficult to make the transition from soldier back to civilian. He was forced to abandon an expedition to the Antarctic because of chronic back pain and eventually went home to Newtownards. He became Secretary of the Incorporated Law Society of Northern Ireland, but found the work mundane. His drinking sessions often led to the police being called, but matters were usually smoothed over before things went too far. He died on 15 December 1955, when his Reilly sports car crashed into a lorry that was parked unlit on the roadside near his home. His funeral was the biggest ever seen in Newtownards. In 1997, a bronze statue of the Colonel was unveiled in the town. Many of his old comrades attended the ceremony, including Johnny

Cooper, Reg Seekings, Jim Almonds and Jimmy Storie. Mayne has been depicted as something of a 'flawed hero' by his critics despite having won the DSO (four times), the Croix de Guerre and the Legion d'Honneur. A recommendation to award him the Victoria Cross fell on deaf ears after the war, possibly due to his unruly off-duty antics. The campaign to posthumously award him the VC goes on.

REG SEEKINGS parachuted into France on D-Day with the rest of the SRS. He married his wife Monica in 1945 and for the next nine years they ran a pub in Ely, his hometown. They then emigrated to Southern Rhodesia where he was a police inspector, before returning home and settling in Suffolk. He died on 16 March 1999.

SARAH O'DOWD overcame her heartbreak, and lived on in good health for another three decades. She died in 1972, aged ninety (James having passed away in 1960 following a farm accident). Joe, Chris's last surviving sibling, died in 2005.

Appendix

Documents relating to Chris O'Dowd

Report in Chris O'Dowd's handwriting.

...ing at Barani.
Went with Capt McDermot
after straffed MT on
the Barani — Matruh
road blew up the
line and destroyed
four machine gun posts
south of Barani

Citation for Chris O'Dowd's Military Medal.

TOP SECRET

Unit: IRISH GUARDS
    (attached to 1st Special Air Service Regiment).

Regtl No.: 2719054

Rank and Name: CORPORAL Christopher O'Dowd.

Action for which commended: Cpl. O'Dowd has taken part in five successful operations with the 1st S.A.S. Regiment. In all these operations, he has shown consistent bravery and steadiness.

At FUKA aerodrome on the 8th July 1942 he assisted to destroy 30 enemy aircraft.

While engaged on a raid on Benghasi on 14th September 1942 he was in the last vehicle to leave covering the withdrawal by accurate and sustained machine gun fire which drew the defenders fire from the main withdrawing party.

On 23rd October, 1942 he was the senior N.C.O. of the raiding party which attacked an enemy convoy driving from SIWA to MERSA MATRUH, assisting in destroying four Lancias.

On 26th October, 1942 he assisted in blowing up the railway line west of MERSA MATRUH.

On 1st November, 1942 he was the senior N.C.O. in a party of six which straffed traffic at SIDI BARRANI and then attacked a railway siding capturing eighteen prisoners, four machine guns, blowing up the railway line and destroying wireless equipment.

Letter from the Palace, inviting Chris's brother, Martin, to collect his medal at St James's.

CENTRAL CHANCERY OF
THE ORDERS OF KNIGHTHOOD,
ST. JAMES' PALACE, S.W.1.

13th January, 1945.

CONFIDENTIAL

Sir,

I have the honour to inform you that your attendance is requested at Buckingham Palace at 10.15 o'clock a.m., on Tuesday, the 20th February, 1945, in order that you may receive from The King, on behalf of your father, the Military Medal awarded to his son, the late Lance-Sergeant Christopher O'Dowd, Irish Guards.

DRESS : Service Dress, Civil Defence Uniform, Morning Dress or dark Lounge Suit.

You may be accompanied by one relation only, who must be a blood relation of the deceased (children under seven may not attend) and I shall be glad if you will complete the enclosed form and return it to me immediately. Two third class return railway vouchers will be forwarded to you (if resident outside the London area) if you so desire, and I shall be glad if you will give the details required on the enclosed form.

This letter should be produced on entering the Palace as no further cards of admission will be issued.

I am, Sir,

Your obedient Servant,

(Signed) W. H. STOCKLEY.
Major.

Secretary.

Martin O'Dowd, Esq.,

Official form sent with Chris's private property after his death.

Army Form B. 104—126.

Any further letter on this subject should be addressed to :
Officer I/c *Irish Guards* Records, and the following No. quoted.

Station............

Date............ 19......

To *J. O'DOWD*
Badgurfort
Shrule, Co Galway
Eire

From [stamp: IRISH GUARDS RECORDS 30 MAR 1944 BIRDCAGE WALK]

SIR OR MADAM,

I am directed to forward the undermentioned articles of private property of the late No. *2719054* Rank *L/Sgt*

Name *O'Dowd*

Regiment *Irish Guards*

and would ask that you will kindly acknowledge receipt of the same on the form overleaf :—

2 Wrist Watches 95 Straps
1 Rosary
Correspondence

These are the only articles at present forthcoming, but should any further articles be received at any time they will be duly forwarded.

Yours faithfully,

for Officer in charge of Records.

Wt.30245/1254 500m 9/39 KJL/8819 Gp.698/3 Forms B/104-126/2

159

Bibliography

Asher, Michael, *The Regiment: The Real Story of the SAS*, 2008. Penguin Books, London.

Bradford, R. and Dillon, M., *Rogue Warrior of the SAS*, 1987. John Murray Publishers, UK.

Carey, Donal, *Gortjordan N.S: At the Heart of the Community*. A history of Gortjordan school, 1996.

Crawford, Steve, *The SAS Encyclopedia*, 1996. Simon & Schuster, London.

Deakins, William, *The Lame One: Sod this for a Game of Soldiers*, 2001. Arthur H. Stockwell.

James, Malcolm (Malcolm Pleydell), *Born of the Desert*, 2006. Greenhill Books, London.

McClean, Stewart, *SAS: The History of the Special Raiding Squadron 'Paddy's Men'*, 2005. Spellmount, Gloucestershire.

Marrinan, Patrick, *Colonel Paddy*, 1968. H.J. Lappin, Ulster Press.

Mortimer, Gavin, *Stirling's Men*, 2004. Weidenfeld & Nicholson, London.

Ross, Hamish, *Paddy Mayne*, 2003. Sutton Publishing.

Stephens, Gordon, *The Originals: The Secret History of the Birth of the SAS*, 2005. Ebury Press, London

Verney, Peter, *The Micks: The Story of the Irish Guards*, 1970. Pan Books, London.

SAS The Originals (DVD), Bite Yer Legs Productions, 2006.

Index

164

166

167